BE MY GUEST

BE MY GUEST

Vivian Anderson Hall

MOODY PRESS

CHICAGO

ISBN: 0-8024-0480-4

Printed in the United States of America

To
Mother and Dad,
who share what they have
with the people whom God sends,
at the time He chooses to send them.

CONTENTS

FOREWORD

Christian hospitality is not a matter of choice; it is not a matter of money; it is not a matter of age, social standing, sex, or personality. Christian hospitality is a matter of obedience to God.

Both Old and New Testaments clearly exhort God's people to exercise the sanctified sharing of hearth and home, of bed and board, and of themselves as opportunities to bless and be blessed. To disregard or shun this biblical call to hospitality is to rob not only oneself but also the Body of Christ of both evangelistic and nurturing ministries at home and around the world. Wherever there is even one child of God there is the responsibility to practice Christian hospitality.

Be My Guest analyzes the wide scope and challenges of this ministry. As pastor's wife, mother, homemaker, church and community worker, and especially—wherever she goes—as a channel of Christian concern for people, Vivian Hall writes with wisdom and sensitivity. Her book is for everyone—young and old, single and married, rich and poor, men and women. It is for guests as well as for hosts and hostesses. It is for congregations as well as for individual lay persons. It is for veteran preachers and their wives as well as for seminarians and fledgling ministers and their spouses.

Be My Guest is far more than a how-to compendium, although many practical helps, even recipes and blow-by-blow guidelines for church dinners are included. How to entertain is

9

not the book's primary objective; far more significant is the why of Christian hospitality from which awareness will then issue also of its who, when, and even where.

Honestly and prayerfully applied, the biblical principles of Christian hospitality expounded and illustrated in this book will enliven persons, homes, and churches for greater communication and demonstration of the gospel.

HELGA HENRY
(MRS. CARL F. H. HENRY)

ACKNOWLEDGMENTS

In a real sense, *Be My Guest* has been a community project.

My church family has encouraged me, prayed for me, and protected my time from interruptions.

My own family has had a part. Jan, Anne, and Chris kept prodding me and often did my other work so that I could write. Beth read and edited the first draft. Jerry kept my theology in order and was involved in every part of this "new project" of mine.

The editors and staff at Moody Press have worked patiently with me.

Some of my friends have become personally involved. Ellen Kok started the whole thing by asking me to teach a lesson on hospitality; then, along with her husband, Gerry, she prayed for me daily as I wrote.

Sharon Richitt encouraged me to "get going" and backed up her encouragement by typing for me.

Jerry Anderson and Eleanor Fietch became my proofreaders.

Veda Hays typed the final manuscript.

Helga Henry graciously agreed to read the manuscript and to write the foreword.

Holly Hodne joined me in proofreading galleys.

To each of these people, who willingly "got involved," I say, "Thank you with love."

INTRODUCTION

"But I don't have the gift of hospitality."

Is that what you are thinking as you pick up this book? If it is, this book is for you. I do not think I have the "gift of hospitality" either. I do, however, know that God commands his children to be "given to hospitality" (Romans 12:13) and that He challenges us to show our love for Him by keeping His commandments. (John 14:15).

Many people have said to me, "Oh, it's easy for you to have company. You have the gift of hospitality." But do I? If I were to follow my natural inclination (my old nature), I would have very little company. After all, company uses up my limited energy; it devours my time; and it does interesting things to my bank balance. Left to do what comes naturally, I would choose solitude to company at least nine days out of ten.

No, I do not believe that I have the gift of hospitality—in fact I am not sure that there is such a gift. The Scripture commands us not to neglect hospitality to strangers (Hebrews 13:2), and to practice, or pursue, hospitality (Romans 12:13). In Romans 12, hospitality pops up in the middle of a list of practices that are obviously meant for all Christians.

God's Word never states that hospitality is the work of those who have the gift of hospitality. It never lists hospitality in the various lists of gifts God bestows upon His children. I have come to believe that just as we are commanded to "be witnesses," we are also commanded to "be given to hospitality."

13

To really fulfill either of these commandments with maximum success we must practice them together.

We of the Christian community have gotten ourselves into trouble because we have let the world push us into its hospitality mold. We call having company "entertaining," and that is what too many of us do. We have company to display our abilities (culinary or otherwise), to build up our egos (bigger and better than the Joneses), and to pay our social debts (we have to have them because they had us). In this framework, entertaining can become a "pain in the neck" at best, and for many it becomes a form of sheer torture.

May I suggest that when we keep the commandment to be witnesses, we share with others what we know about God's love; and when we keep the commandment to be hospitable, we express God's love by sharing what we have. God never asks His children to do the impossible, but He tells us to be hospitable. Therefore, we who have accepted God's love have the ability to share what we have with the people God sends into our lives at the time He chooses to send them. And that is obeying the hospitality commandment.

The skills that make this obedience to the hospitality commandment easier are skills that can be learned. I was fortunate to learn many of these skills in my childhood. But I have adult Christian friends who minister effectively in the area of hospitality, yet they had very little opportunity to practice hospitality in their parental homes. It is never too late to learn how to keep God's commandment to be "given to hospitality" or to become more effective as we keep this commandment.

If you do not have the "gift of hospitality," do not worry about it—just begin to share what you have with those God sends into your life at the time that He sends them. When you do this, sooner or later someone will say to you, "Oh, but it's easy for you to have company. You have the gift of hospitality!"

Part One

GET READY FOR COMPANY

*Watch over your heart with all diligence,
For from it flow the springs of life.*

PROVERBS 4:23

1

HOME—GOD'S CREATION

When God created Adam He gave him a home, an environment to live in. That home was a garden, complete and perfect, a beautiful place to live. Then God created Eve. Adam and Eve were a family, living in a home decorated by the master Creator.

Even before sin entered the world, God's command to Adam was to "dress" the garden—to take care of that home he had been given. God did not say, however, to be sure that the lily opened its blossom only during the night hours or that the grapevine could only grow when it was all alone. Life was to unfold in the garden home when people were watching as well as when there was solitude.

God made Eden as a home for his children, a place to live, to work, and to play. It was a place in which to express love and laughter. In this garden home obedience brought joy, and disobedience brought fear.

When we plan our homes, this first home, created by God, should be our model. Yet, I can almost hear some of you saying, "My home is no Garden of Eden. I live in a dormitory, a small house trailer, a noisy apartment, a tract house in the suburbs, or a farmhouse twenty miles from nowhere. Really, lady, it isn't Eden!"

Maybe not, but you need to understand that whether your home is a tent, a cottage, or an earthly mansion, it is a gift to you from God— just as much as Eden was God's gift to Adam.

If God gave it to you, it is good. It is His place for you right now, and He expects you to "dress" it, bring out its best qualities. You are to live in it, to love in it, to laugh in it, to pray in it, and to serve Him in it in a ministry of hospitality.

Our home is sometimes an art studio, a carpenter's shop, a concert hall, a bakery, a craft studio, a day nursery, a short order restaurant, a pet shop, a hospital, a retreat, and many other things. Our God is a creator, and those of us who call this place "home" were created in His image. We like to "mimic" our heavenly Father by being miniature creators. We also like to enjoy His very special creations like babies and grandparents, blue-eyed kittens and boisterous puppies, green grass and blue skies, rain on the roof and sunshine spilling through white curtains. Our house is a sanctuary where we worship God, and to the outside observer it often takes on the characteristics of Grand Central Station. It is not elegant but it is most adequate, and you are welcome to come and share it with us.

You may find a little sawdust or the smell of home-baked bread present. I am sure that you can learn to enjoy the scales being practiced on the piano when they are followed by the music of Bach. You will be welcomed by inquisitive barks and enquiring meows along with human voices, and you may come into the kitchen and pour yourself a cup of coffee while I fix us something to eat. We do not have any "help," so I may ask you to join in and get the work done so that we can visit on the patio or by the fireplace a little later.

We are not the Statler-Hilton complete with room service. God did not ask us to be that. He just asked us to create a home where His little children could grow up assured of our love and acceptance. He gave us a place to renew our strength in quiet times, to stretch our abilities to create, and to enjoy His creation with each other.

He also asked us to let Him feel free to ask His friends to drop in sometimes and to share our home life. My God has the most amazing assortment of friends. They come in many colors, sizes, and shapes; each one is different, and each one is special. He wants to give us the privilege of knowing some of these friends of His.

Sometimes I complain, "But, Lord, I'm too tired today."

He whispers, "My strength is made perfect in your weakness."

"But, Lord, my back aches."

He reminds me, "My burden is light. Where did you pick up that heavy one?"

"But, Lord, I don't have time today."

He says, "If you will reverence me, I will add the needed hours to your day."

All right, Lord, it's Your home, too. Bring me Your friends so that I can enjoy them. But please stay close and help me to remember that You are my strength; we're in this together.

2

WHY ME, GOD?

"My house is too dirty."

"I don't have time—I'm so busy."

"I'm going to wait until the children are older."

"I don't know what to say to people."

"My house is too small."

"They have children, and I don't want my things spoiled."

"My health won't permit it."

"My mother lives with us, you know."

"It's inconvenient now."

"I can't. I work."

These are just a few of the many reasons I have heard, and have sometimes used, for not accepting the opportunity to extend hospitality. "If you wait for perfect conditions, you will never get anything done" (Ecclesiastes 11:4, TLB*) is the very good observation of wise King Solomon. Life just is not made up of ideals. Ever since Eve yielded to the serpent in Eden, living conditions on this earth have been less than perfect.

When God commands us to be hospitable, He is not asking us to be perfect; He is asking us to share our imperfect selves and our imperfect homes with the people He chooses to send to us. He will not ask us to share what we do not have, but He will ask us to use what we have. Furthermore, He will make our resources go an incredibly long way when we yield to Him and seek to live by His rules.

*The Living Bible.

20

"Let love of the brethren continue" (Hebrews 13:1). God commands us to reach out to those of the household of faith. "Do not neglect to show hospitality to strangers" (Hebrews 13:2). He continues showing us that Christlike hospitality is not limited to those we know and are sure we will feel comfortable with.

The first incident involving "hospitality to strangers" that I remember occurred when I was a small child living with my parents on a northern Minnesota farm. The house was small, and it became smaller in winter when we shut off the parts of it that could not be heated by the woodburning stove in the living room. Most of our living was then done in two rooms, a bedroom converted into a winter kitchen, and the living room. Upstairs were bedrooms where we did not linger out of bed any longer than necessary.

At this home a stranger knocked at the door. He was a young man who identified himself as an American Sunday School Union missionary assigned to minister to our community. He was welcomed warmly. Mother quickly changed her menu to make supper a company meal, and a bed was made ready for him. Now, some forty years later, this man and his family are still counted among my parents' close friends. He was a stranger only once. Ever after he was a friend who came regularly and ministered to their needs, even as they ministered to his.

Looking back to that first visit, I am sure that it was a sacrifice of time and material that my parents made that day, though I doubt if they ever thought of it in that light. They shared what was available, graciously—a simple meal eaten by the light of a kerosene lamp, a lantern to find the path to the outdoor facilities, and a bed well dressed with Mother's handmade quilts. But more important than any of these was the love that they gave to this man who was called of God to minister in that northland.

I was unaware of it at the time, but I was given a real lesson in Christian hospitality that day. I have so much more of this world's goods than my parents had at that time. This compels me to share with those whom God sends to me even if they are strangers. The writer to the Hebrews encourages such sharing with these words: "And do not neglect doing good and sharing; for with such sacrifices God is pleased" (Hebrews 13:16).

God commands us to share the things He has entrusted to us. He commands us to share the love that He has placed in our hearts with others of His family. Yet we seem to drag our heels and use worn-out excuses for our disobedience.

Why are we so afraid to share God's goodness to us with others? Are we so selfish that we want it all for ourselves? Or are we so lazy that we do not want to be bothered? Maybe these are reasons for disobedience, but I do not believe either of these is the main reason many of the Christians I know are not keeping the hospitality commandment. They are neither selfish nor lazy—they are afraid! Afraid that they cannot "do it right." Afraid that they will offend because of the inadequacy of their homes. Afraid that they are imposing upon their potential guests. Afraid because they might not be able to do it as well as Mrs. Jones does.

Do you not know that God does not give us a spirit of fear or inadequacy? God's Spirit in us produces love, joy, peace, and sound reasoning (see 2 Timothy 1:7). If our fears are not of God, they can come only from Satan whose prime objective with regard to the Christian is to hinder him from fulfilling God's commandments and receiving God's blessing. You do not need to yield to your fears, for God's Spirit is stronger than the spirit of Satan. When you yield to the Lord, cry out, "Help, Lord," and He will show you how to overcome your fears and to fulfill His hospitality commandment.

3

HELP, LORD!

Why am I so afraid of people, Lord? Why do I not want to share my life as You have commanded? Could it be that I don't really understand what You meant when You commanded me to be hospitable?

Too often we are afraid because we are measuring our own lives by the lives of those Christians who have different gifts than ours and whose talents and spiritual maturity are different from our own. We have put ourselves in competition with our Christian friends. This is wrong. There is no room for competition in the Christian community. Our commandment is: "Live together in harmony, live together in love, as though you had only one mind and spirit between you" (Philippians 2:2, Phillips*). We are not to compete, but we are to think of the well-being of others with the same concern that we have for ourselves (see Philippians 2:1-4).

Competition is the devil's delight, and he loves to stifle our spirit of hospitality by getting us to compete with one another. "Bigger and better," he whispers. (*Lord, help me not to listen.*) We consider inviting a person to our home who has more of this world's goods than we do, and Satan informs us, "He might be uncomfortable in your poor home." We turn to the one who has less than we do, and he suggests, "He will be ill at ease in your lovely home." We consider the friend who is our equal, and he reminds us, "He owes you an invitation, and he

*The New Testament in Modern English.

23

will feel bad if you invite him again before he has fulfilled his obligation."

All too often we listen to this enemy while forgetting the leveling effect of Calvary. As Christians we are all members of the same family, different from each other as brothers and sisters always are, but united because we have the same heritage. We are sinners saved by the grace of God, adopted by the same heavenly Father. When we come to really understand that we are all members of the same family, working together toward the same goal—to be conformed to the image of Christ—we will have no reason to be afraid of each other, even when our life-styles are different.

We are sometimes afraid to share ourselves and our possessions because we do not really know who we are. Our minds have been saturated by the implications of commercial enterprises that say we are missing the mark if we do not use this product, or study this philosophy, or drink this beverage. We are being programmed to think that we are inadequate beings. In a sense this is true: we are sinners, but so is every other person who walks the face of the earth today. This fact does not make us inferior to one another.

How does God think of us? He created us in His own image (see Genesis 1:27). We are made according to God's blueprint, and He read it correctly. When God creates, it is good. God is a perfectionist, and He made no mistake on you or me. He made us just as we are so that He could enjoy fellowship with us and so that we could bring glory to Him.

But in Adam we sinned, and we have all been sinning ever since. *It is all over,* we think. *We have lost our perfection, and we have lost our fellowship.* Yes, we were the losers because of sin, but the wonder of it is that God did not decide to discard us and start again—He chose to renew us and to rebuild His image in us. This is redemption. "It is God himself who has made us what we are and given us new lives from Christ Jesus; and long ages ago he planned that we should spend these lives in helping others" (Ephesians 2:10, TLB).

The God who made me and who is remaking me knows that I am an imperfect being, and yet He planned that my imperfect life should be spent ministering to others. It is God's plan, and all of His plans are good. I do not need to be afraid of my inadequacies because God took them into account when He planned the ministry of hospitality for me.

Just what did God mean when He commanded that I should minister to those of the household of faith and that I should meet the needs of the stranger He sends to my door? Is it a seven-course meal and room service that He had in mind? I do not think so—if it were, I would be afraid, too!

I have come to believe that Christian hospitality is a simple sharing. I have an orange and you are hungry—I give you a little more than half of it. You come to my door needing a bed—I put clean sheets on the bed and invite you to use it. You need a ride to the doctor's office—I have a car and I take you. You come discouraged, and I remember that "good advice satisfies like a good meal!" so I send God an SOS for an appropriate bit of His wisdom to share with you.

True hospitality is sharing what you are and what you have, without thought of personal gain. It does not require that you spend money or energy that you do not have in order to impress your guest. It does ask that you share what you have and what you are with those to whom God has planned for you to minister.

As we share in this way, God increases our abilities and often our material means so that our ministry can be more effective. This, however, is God's part. Our part is to live in the "now," content with His provisions (Hebrews 13:5), secure in our identity as children of God (1 John 3:1), doing the very best that we can with what we have now, and not comparing our performance with that of others (Galatians 6:4).

When are we to start? Now. Where are we to begin? In the place in which God has put us now. How are we to know what to do? "But if any of you lacks wisdom, let him ask of God, who gives to all men generously and without reproach, and it will be given to him. But let him ask in faith without any doubting, for the one who doubts is like the surf of the sea driven and tossed by the wind" (James 1:5-6).

4

HOUSEKEEPING FOR THE GLORY OF GOD

Though I can and do offer hospitality to people when I am away from home, my central base of operation is home. My God is interested in how I care for my home just as He was interested in how Adam and Eve cared for Eden.

God never really got into the fanatical end of the "women's lib" movement, though I am sure that He approves of fair treatment for His women. He has never considered homemaking an inferior profession. Homemaking is of course a much bigger job than housekeeping, but any good homemaker can tell you that housekeeping must be a part of it if you are to be successful.

God seems to have created women with a nesting instinct, the desire to improve their living conditions, and to add beauty to their surroundings. Whether we hold a nine-to-five job or make homemaking our only career, we are happiest when our home base reflects our own personalities. The keeping of the home is part of the work that God has planned for us. Because it is God's plan, it is good.

God has a plan; do I? do you? Or do we just plod through another mountain of dirty laundry, another sink full of dirty dishes, and another round of dusty furniture? God never intended for me to dwell in the dirt. He gave me a mind so that I can order my day to take care of removing the dirt. As a result I can enjoy fluffy yellow towels that smell good, sparkling clean drinking glasses, and the glow of well-waxed furniture.

Every occupation on this earth has some routine tasks con-

27

nected with it, and housekeeping is no exception. These tasks can be accomplished well in a minimum amount of time and, in the case of housekeeping, often at our convenience. When we fail to plan, these same tasks can eat up most of our time. Do you have a plan, or are you just letting your days happen?

Is your theme song "When I get my house in order I'll have company?" If it is, and if this is your emphasis, I doubt whether you will ever get around to "being hospitable." Now do not misunderstand me. I believe that a reasonably clean, well-ordered house is honoring to God, but when your house keeps you from doing what God has commanded, something is wrong.

How do you begin your day? Is it, "Ugh, another day of those dirty D's (dishes, diapers, and dust)." Or do you begin by inspecting the day God has prepared for you, thanking Him for the sunshine, rain, or snow along with your thanks for the work that He has planned for you this day?

Do you give the gift of this day back to God for Him to use for His glory, or do you hang on to it, determined to have it your way. An attitude of thanksgiving (or of complaint) in the morning often sets the tone for the entire day. It may sound trite, but it really does help to begin each day right. Of course we all slip up here at times, but as soon as we become aware of an unthankful spirit we can, with God's help, change that attitude.

When you commit your day to the Lord you may be surprised to find out what He has planned for you. He may send a special friend to minister to you, or He may suggest that you dig in and clean out that hall closet. You know the one; you have been avoiding it for a month or so now. God knows that the mess in there has been hindering your peace of mind, so He is urging you to do it now!

It amazes me how quickly those distasteful jobs that we keep putting off can be done. I found out the other day that I could wash all the woodwork in the living room and dining room in three hours, and I had been dreading the task for three weeks.

Just how do I let God plan my day? With paper and pen in my hand. My most successful days are planned-out days when I list things that need to be accomplished and things that would be nice to do. Here is a copy of one of my day plans.

"We can make our plans, but the final outcome is in God's hands."
Proverbs 16:1, TLB

Have to Jobs

Kitchen cleanup
Put house in order
Bake cookies for Jerry's class
Vacuum first floor
Grocery shop
Spray roses

Maybe Jobs

Finish ironing
Sew knit top for Anne
Work on chapter five
Give dog a bath

Phone Calls

Church office
Carol

Letters

Birthday card to Sally
Note to Shirl
Thank you to Katherine

Dinner Tonight

Meat Balls
Potato salad*   Spinach
Tomato and Cucumber Salad*
Cookies
   (*Prepare during kitchen cleanup time)

For me, the best time to make this list is right after breakfast when I have had a short period of time reading and thinking about God's Word. If I do this then, I am more attuned to God's ideas for my day and less tangled up with pressures that come from the world around me. This day sheet is a guide for my day but is very subject to change. By the end of this day my day plan looked like this:

Have to Jobs

Kitchen cleanup
Put house in order
Bake cookies for Jerry's class
Vacuum first floor

Grocery shop	(Marie came to visit.
Spray roses	Had Jerry pick up
	eggs and milk.)

Phone Calls

Church office
Carol
   Got seven calls today

Dinner Tonight

Meat Balls
Potato salad   Spinach
Tomato and Cucumber Salad
Cookies

Maybe Jobs

Finish ironing

Sew knit top for Anne

Work on chapter five
   (2 hours)
Give dog a bath—
   Thanks, Anne!

Letters

Birthday card to Sally

Note to Shirl

Thank you to Katherine

The Lord sent company;
added homemade rolls
from the freezer, some
pickles and ice cream, and
had a good time.

The boxed-in things did not get done and so will go on to-morrow's list. The day was committed to the Lord, and He knew that Marie needed a little time at my kitchen table more than I needed to grocery shop or garden. He had planned the extra surprise blessing of good friends coming to town, so I shall sew and write to Shirl tomorrow or maybe next week. In the meantime I can thank Him for a dinner menu that easily expanded to feed three guests as well as my family. We were so blessed by their coming, and I think they were, too.

My day plan is a flexible guideline to my day. If I try to make it more than that I can easily become frustrated, for my life, like that of any wife and mother, is full of interruptions. However, if I do not make this plan, I have found that I will usually work harder and get less done. I need goals. You may use an entirely different system—that is fine, just as long as you have a system that works for you.

If we live without a plan the result is frustration and confusion. We do not know what we are doing well and where we need improvement. Galatians 6:4 says, "But let every man prove his own work, and then shall he have rejoicing in himself alone, and not in another" (KJV*).

We are to keep track of ourselves, competing only with our past record. So that I may know if I am a better housekeeper this year than I was last year, I need records. They do not have to be elaborate, but I need them as a measuring stick. When I find there is improvement, I have the right to enjoy my accomplishment. This gives me the dignity and self respect that makes housekeeping enjoyable.

Along with my day plan I also have a goals book that covers many areas of my life, including housekeeping. In this notebook I list the things I want to accomplish this week, this month, and this year. I also have some things in it that will take a lifetime to accomplish. To date I do not believe I have ever completed any one of those lists in the given period of time. This does not frustrate me, for I get a lot more done when I set my goals too high than when I set them so low that they are easy to reach.

Housekeeping is made up of daily necessities like cooking, cleaning, marketing, washing, and ironing, but this is only part of housekeeping. There is the "dressing" part, which to me is sheer delight. How can I make my home comfortable and attractive to each member of my family? We should not be caught up in dressing our homes to surpass the Joneses or to please Aunt Sue (unless she is a live-in-member of the family). Houses are basically for the people that actually live in them, and they should be made as comfortable as possible for those people.

*King James Version.

Periodically we need to evaluate the dressing of our homes to be sure that we are meeting the current needs.

A new baby is on the way, and the extra room becomes a nursery, even if the extra room is only a closet. A few years later we need to realize that no school child needs a nursery and that teenagers thrive on privacy. When the children grow up and leave home, Dad can have a den, and Mother can have a sewing room that she can shut the door on. Yes, I know it may seem strange to give up the children's rooms, but it will help make your days more enjoyable when you get used to the idea. It will also assure your children that you respect their grown-up status.

As soon as you can, if you are committed to a ministry of hospitality, you will want to set aside "God's room," more commonly called the guest room. This is not to say that you will not have house guests until you have this special room, but nothing helps hospitality feelings like a room that is always ready for the guest God sends.

I would not attempt to tell you just how you should dress your home. Color, texture, and furniture styles and arrangements are individual things and should reflect the taste of the persons who live there. I would urge you to study what your family likes, consider what you can afford, find out what you are comfortable with, and then go to it with gusto—for the glory of God.

Remember that God created everything from the desert to the jungle—beautifully. Do not be tricked into thinking that to please Him your home must be of stereotyped decor—His imagination is endless. Do not be afraid to ask for God's help as you create your background for family living and hospitality. When your decorating consultant is the master Creator, interesting things just have to happen, and when you enjoy your home you will be much more comfortable saying, "Please be my guest."

5

BE MY GUEST

To me, a phrase that holds real magic is *var så god*. It is the Scandinavian invitation to come to the table, and the most common translation I can get for it is "Be my guest." Most of the people of Scandinavian heritage that I have known enjoy being hospitable. It is a learned habit that permeates the Christian Scandinavian community. The food may be simple or fancy. It makes no difference—it is the attitude that makes it special. To me, *var så god* says, "I am happy to share with you that which I have," and that is what Christian hospitality is all about.

How do you choose whom you will have as your guest? At our house often we do not do the choosing. We have let the Lord know that we have an "open house" policy, and He sends the people of His choosing. We have also asked God for His protection so that we do not get more than we can physically handle and so that we do not misspend our hospitality energy.

God has a marvelous scheduling ability. We realized this more fully during the bicentennial summer. During that summer we had six weeks of continual houseguests. There was not a serious overlap, everyone had a bed, and there were enough chairs to go around. The average length of stay of these guests was four and one-half days and, though the outgoing guests often changed the sheets for the next company, the scheduling was perfect. Only two of these families had been specifically invited by us. God scheduled those He sent around the dates

33

that these special friends were with us, and we were able to really enjoy everyone who came.

We do give personal invitations to many people to come and see us for a meal, for a cup of coffee, or for a few days. God gives us His wisdom in this as in any other area of life. The church my husband pastors is not large, but it is too big for us to entertain on a regular basis everyone who attends. Apart from the occasional "open house" to which everyone is invited, welcomed, and expected, we must rely on God's Spirit to show us whom we should invite into our home. Sometimes we invite those with special ministries, when God's work is helped by our having a little more time together (this includes special committees and boards within the church). Often invitations go to husbands whose wives are out of town or to people who live alone. Sometimes we are aware of a special need and choose to invite a certain person, and sometimes we are not aware of a special need, but God just seems to nudge us and say, "What about asking So-and-So to dinner?" Other times when I did not really plan to have anyone, I find myself saying, "Would you like to come home and eat with us?" When we are willing, God is very able to provide the right guests at the right time.

A large portion of our hospitality is extended to those of God's servants who happen to be visiting in our city for a period of time. It has been our policy to make our guest room available to fellow Christians who need a place to stay when the Lord brings their need to our attention. Often these are people who are strangers to us. This may seem a bit scary to you if you have not been involved in this type of hospitality.

God has proved to us over and over again that He can work out all things to His glory and our good when we trust Him. I cannot think of a single instance when we have had to refuse someone because of lack of room or of a single time when God has sent us more than we have had the physical strength to care for.

When you decide to extend this type of hospitality you are giving your faith a wonderful chance to grow. This is what you are asking God to do:

- To send the people of His choice
- To choose the time that they should come and to decide how long they should stay
- To protect you from those who would misuse your hospitality
- To provide the material means necessary to minister to these people
- To give you spiritual insight to know how to meet both the physical and spiritual needs of your guests
- To keep your own spirit open to the blessings God has planned that you receive from these guests.

I can say emphatically that God has never failed us in any of these areas. Because we have found Him so dependable it has become more and more enjoyable to participate in the ministry of hospitality. When we have chosen to obey, our blessings have far outweighed the effort that we have expended. Our minds have been expanded, our vision of God's work broadened, and our friends have multiplied in a way we could never have imagined when we began our home twenty-seven years ago. When we obey, God blesses, and I have come to believe that all the company that God sends to us is very special.

Part Two

THE GUEST LIST

*Be hospitable to one another
without complaint.*
1 PETER 4:9

6

FAMILY FIRST

If your hospitality is to be successful in the full sense of the word, it must begin at home. In your own family unit, the principles of hospitality need to be practiced continually. Since hospitality is basically the sharing of yourself and your possessions, it is imperative that this sharing begin in your own home with your own family.

The expression of hospitality within the family unit can take many forms. Mother and Dad will of course set the example for their children to follow, and they will encourage their children to participate. Mother can plan an extra good meal with a well-appointed table, every now and then, for her most important guests—Dad and "the kids." Dad can be the chef on occasion and Mother the guest of honor. If Dad is not the world's best cook, who cares?—it is the idea that counts. The children, while they are little, can plan tea parties and picnics with pretend food. This is an experience every parent is entitled to. As they grow older, real food will replace the pretend menus, and the meals can become very exotic on some occasions.

One large family that I know cannot afford to "eat out" very often, and when they do the food is usually hamburgers. But each payday all year long, Dad tucks just a little away so that he can extend a special kind of hospitality to his family once a year. For Mother's Day he makes a reservation at a very nice restaurant, and they all go out to eat.

Sometimes teenagers with jobs can take their parents out for dinner. This will be a grand occasion, even if the destination is McDonald's, for the children are learning the joys of giving hospitality. Also, every child needs some solitary hospitality from each of his parents. One of these special times came for our daughter when her father took her as his date to a real, bona fide adult banquet.

When either Mother or Dad has to be gone for the evening meal, special hospitality can be extended to the children by the parent at home. Something that is different from the regular routine can be planned. It could be pizza eaten in front of the fireplace or hot dogs roasted on sticks over coals in the barbecue grill. What it is, is not as important as the fact that you made the effort to make a good time out of what might have been a lonesome time.

Every child should, on occasion, witness the sight of Mother getting ready to go out on a date wth Dad. This is important hospitality that married couples should include in their schedules and budgets. It is sometimes fun when Mother reverses the role and takes Dad somewhere. The child who witnesses the preparations for such occasions will find security in knowing that Mom and Dad enjoy each other.

Parents can make this time a treat for their stay-at-home small children by hiring a favorite babysitter and planning a menu for them that includes food the little ones really enjoy. Suggest activities to your babysitter that will make the time pass quickly for everybody.

Parenting as a full-time task is one job that we need to work ourselves out of. Successful parenting means that the day will come when your child is willing and ready to leave home. Then you have the opportunity to extend a different type of hospitality to him.

We love to have our children come home to visit. We have been known to encourage such visits by sending gasoline credit cards and prepaid tickets. Although we cannot always clear the schedule when they come, we do all we can to loosen it. We like to set aside quiet times to catch up on what is happening in their lives, to plan some activities of mutual interest, and to extend hospitality to some of their friends. As we do this we also try to leave them plenty of free time. Our very best friends are our now grown-up children, and they are our favorite company.

Almost every set of parents comes complete with two families—his and hers. These are the people who are often best qualified to teach your children that having company is fun. Children can help get ready for a visit from their grandparents, a favorite aunt and/or uncle, or some of the cousins. This may mean that Aunt Mary has a vase full of dandelions on her bedside table. A loving grandson may extend the ultimate in hospitality and let Grandpa sleep with his teddy bear. Please do not discourage these loving acts—Aunt Mary will see the love behind these yellow blossoms, and Grandpa, if he is anything like the grandpas I know, will delight in telling the story of how he got to sleep with Billy's favorite toy.

Your families should be accorded all the courtesy that is extended to any guest who visits you. Along with this should be some extra loving touches that can reach from the elegant to the ridiculous just as long as they say, "We're glad you are here."

My sister once returned from a missionary term in Nigeria to find a large contingency of her family at the local airport with a very long banner that proclaimed, "Welcome home, Auntie Faye." That was special for her, and for some of her little grandnieces and grandnephews it was just about the most exciting thing they had ever done. They did not know it, of course, but for these little children this was a good lesson in being hospitable.

When your families come to visit it is nice to plan some outings, but do be sure to leave plenty of visiting time. Busyness can rob you of that special sharing that is essential to keeping family ties strong. In these days when most of us are separated from at least part of our families by many miles, the visits that you receive from these people can and should be highlights in your life.

Things like meals tucked into the freezer before their arrival can free you to enjoy your guests more while they are with you. Simplicity in living can help a lot. If the visit is short, this is a time when you cancel all the things that are not absolutely essential. Pick up the clutter now and then but turn a blind eye to the fingerprints on the woodwork in the dining room. Pour another cup of coffee or tea and enjoy your guests.

If you have not been involved in the ministry of hospitality, by all means start with your immediate family, today. Move on to your extended families as soon as possible, and then you will be ready to reach out to friends and strangers the world around.

7

SLÄKTING KIN AND CLOSE FRIENDS

"Oh, they are my *släkting* kin," the charming Swedish mother informed me, as she introduced her sister-in-law's family to me. Somehow, that term seemed to make a closer relationship between her and her son's new in-laws.

I like the term, I have used it, and I have heard it used by many of my Swedish friends, but I had never checked out its validity until I began to write this chapter. All the Swedish dictionaries list *släkting* as a word for "relative," but none of them add "kin." My Swedish friends seem to have done something that is not uncommon to bilingual people—they have combined a Swedish word for relative with an English word for relative and have coined a term with a different meaning. I think it is a great expression—*släkting* kin, the relatives of the relatives. These are the people who are not related to you, either by blood ties or by marriage, but who are related to your in-laws.

I want to include this group of people in this book and to couple them with your closest friends. Why this combination? Because close friendships are built on mutual interests, and here we already have, or should have, a mutual interest in our "linking" relative. Your family life can be much more rewarding if you establish good interpersonal relationships with the families of your in-laws.

I often hear young couples talking of the difficulties they have keeping two sets of parents happy. The equal-time question becomes paramount in their minds when they think of parents. When you battle this problem for very long, it sometimes becomes easier just to forget both sets of parents and not have to decide whose turn it is this time. This problem can be avoided if the parents involved will become good friends.

How are good friendships made? By spending time together, by helping each other, by exploring areas of mutual interest, and by being willing to love another person even though he is not perfect. At times we will meet someone and know almost immediately that we would like to have that person for a good friend. Other times we meet someone we think, "I don't really like that person." If circumstances make it necessary, or at least advantageous, for us to spend time with the person who does not appeal to us we will sometimes find to our surprise, that the person we thought we did not like has become a good friend.

It is to be hoped that when you meet the persons who are your *släkting* kin you will like them immediately. If you do not, remember that it is to your advantage to develop a good friendship. This type of a friendship is usually entered into through the door of hospitality. Your friendship will grow as you share what you are and what you have with these people whom God has sent into your life.

We have been fortunate in having a good friendship with our daughter-in-law's parents. When the children are in town and need a bed, where they stay has usually been decided by who has the empty bed, not by whose turn it is this time.

When possible, we combine families for holidays. This can, and often does, include not just our two families but Beth's brother-in-law's family as well. We enjoy making these meals planned potlucks so that no one has to work too hard.

When we, the parents, make plans affecting our mutual children, we confer and try to decide what they would like best. Our lives have been enriched by Beth in many ways, and one of

those ways is by a good friendship with her family. This friendship probably would not have happened if she had not become
our daughter too.

Many times we are separated from one of our *släkting* kin by
distance. We are not able to run over and relate a bit of news
over a cup of coffee or tea. Even when this is the case we need
to make good use of the opportunities that we have to build
good friendships with this group of people whom God has
brought into our lives.

Probably all of us have some very close friends—people with
whom we feel completely at ease. These are the people with
whom we will laugh over little unimportant things, and they are
the people we will cry with when life is not laughable. These are
the ones we spend time with as often as possible, and they are
the people with whom we share mutual hospitality. We have
the freedom to invite ourselves to their houses, and they have
the freedom to invite themselves to ours. We are each, also,
free to say, "Sorry, you can't come today. I have a dentist appointment—how about tomorrow, or next week?"

If these close friends are people you cannot see often, you
will bend and break schedules to spend time with them, even if
it is only thirty minutes in an airport coffee shop between
planes. It is with these good friends that most of us can get our
basic lessons in what real hospitality is. We know that we do
not have to put on a performance in order to be accepted. They
know us with a knowledge that includes our weaknesses, and
they love us just the way we are. When we get out the good
china and plan a gourmet meal for these friends, it is to say,
"We love you; you are important to us." It is not to say, "Look
at our abilities and our possessions."

When these friends come, if we do not have time to do anything but cook hamburgers or send out for a bucket of chicken,
we still welcome them because we love them, and we want to
share the time that we have with them. We know they will

understand that in order to have more time together we have chosen a simple meal.

Every person needs good friendships. A basic ingredient to good friendship is sharing. This sharing includes many areas of your life. It will take your time. It will involve your material possessions. It will cause you to open up your mind and heart to another person.

An important part of your ministry of hospitality is this sharing with good friends. A large measure of your hospitality should be to your good friends, and here you are ministered to even as you minister. Here you gain some of the courage that you need to reach out to other people who have not yet become your friends. As you reach out to your good friends, I hope that included in their number are your *släkting* kin.

8

KATIE CALLS ME GRANDMA

A little blond lady, not quite two, walked into my life one June day and started immediately to call me "Grandma." I have no legal right to that title, but I learned to enjoy playing the role. Katie is the granddaughter of good friends of ours, and her Army dentist daddy had just been assigned to Fort Belvoir for one year. Though the Army sent her daddy here, I have no doubt that God sent Katie especially for me—to be my teacher in the art of hospitality to little people.

My children are taller than I am now, and in recent years I had lost touch with the wonders of being little. I had actually come to find it inconvenient to have small children around. Because I was busy I could usually find ways to avoid this inconvenience. God knew the perfect way to melt this hardening of the heart that was forming in me. Katie was His messenger. With two chubby arms around my neck, soft kisses on the cheek, and a little voice saying, "I love you, Grandma," it was not at all hard to rediscover that entertaining little people is a blessing.

This is a different type of hospitality than we have been talking about, but in God's sight I am sure that it is rated very high. In Matthew 18:6 we are told that it would be better for us to drown than to offend a child. God places a high premium on right treatment of children. I needed to be reminded that my priorities had to be overhauled.

Children are people and deserve as much respect as a person of any other age. This respect means that I will be trustworthy when they share their private thoughts with me. I will not gossip them to adults just because they seem cute or funny to our adult minds.

When I am entertaining a child, I will seek to minister to his needs. He needs a chair high enough to be at comfortable table level when I feed him. He needs a quiet place to rest at naptime, with possibly a teddy bear or special soft blanket to keep him from being lonesome. There should be good books to read together, to expand his awareness of the wonderful world that God has created for him to live in. There should be things to play with and places to run and tumble to use up some of the beautiful supply of energy God has provided him. There should be areas in my home that are reasonably child-proof, where real valuables are out of reach but where there are pretty things that can be looked at and even touched.

Most of the above things can be of makeshift variety. Telephone books will raise a chair to table level, cookie cutters and pots and pans will do for toys, and books can be magazines with bright colored pictures in them.

There is however one thing that you will need to give your little guest that cannot be of a makeshift variety. He needs a generous supply of genuine love and interest. This love will be patient, taking the time to teach right and wrong. When parents are not present, it will find loving, gentle, but firm ways to enforce the boundaries of right. It is a love that will never knowingly contradict the parents' authority, and it will be generous with honest praise whenever possible.

Our ministry of hospitality to small children can pay double dividends by giving their parents mini-vacations from the constant responsibilities of caring for them. In the year that Katie lived in our neighborhood, I had the privilege of spending the night with her while her mommy and daddy went to the hospital to get the new brother that God was sending to live in their family. From time to time after his arrival, Katie and I took care of baby Benjamin so that Mommy and Daddy could have an afternoon to go shopping alone or an evening to go out to dinner. Together we enjoyed this delightful smaller person who was another evidence of God's creative ability.

A couple of years ago I might have thought of this as a sacrificial type of hospitality, but I found out that it was not. I was so amply repaid in immeasurable love from both the children and their parents that I shudder to think of what I would have lost in my growing process if Katie had not adopted me as her substitute grandma for the year that they lived here.

As I write this, Katie and her family are halfway around the world from us, fulfilling the Army's next assignment, but some of the evidences of the lessons she taught me are still here along with her picture. A rideable colonial rocking horse lives in our living room. My husband gave it to me for Christmas last year. There are also handcrafted wooden toys that my children gave me for my birthday. My adult friends are sometimes puzzled by these gifts but all my little friends understand perfectly.

They are the best gifts I could receive because they are for sharing. They also serve as reminders of the importance of not falling back into the pattern of excluding little children from my hospitality ministry. After all, how can I claim to be too busy for boys and girls when Jesus took time—amid a multitude of adults who must have had a multitude of needs—to minister to the little children?

9

KIDS—GROWN UP

Kids in college, kids in the armed services, kids beginning new careers, kids still cleaning Just Married off battered old jalopies or shiny new compacts, and sometimes kids just starting to raise a family—we call them young adults and we love them. When our children were still pedaling tricycles, I began my career of mothering grown-up kids by providing a home away from home for young people who could not go home for their birthdays, holidays, or for Sunday dinner. We believe that some of the energy expended this way will have eternal results.

If you have ever sent a son or a daughter away to a strange city, college dormitory, or an army barracks, you know the rather helpless feeling that overtakes you as a stay-at-home parent. There is a silent prayer or at least a wish that someone with a fair amount of common sense and some love to spare will take an interest in your child—to help him retain and deepen his spiritual values and to be sure that he does not starve to death when he finds himself "broke."

This type of hospitality can bring you love and laughter combined with frustration and heartache. You will get to hear of the dreams and the romances of these young guests and also the problems that come when these dreams and romances do not measure up to their expectations. There is ample opportunity to teach spiritual principles as you dispense love, cookies, and mild reprimands. When you meet the need for mothering in one young person, you will soon find that he or she has friends. I remember coming home from work one day to find that one of my acquired clan had at least six friends, and that they were all enjoying a televised football game in our living room. We had a lot of spaghetti and laughter at our house that night.

We do not usually treat these young people as company—in fact we treat them like temporary members of the family. We love them, scold them, praise them, feed them, and put them to work. If they are financially able, we let them bring dessert for dinner or the ground beef for hamburgers sometimes. If they have been contributing members of their own families they will enjoy contributing to the well-being of their substitute family. If they have not learned to contribute at home, we believe that now is the time to begin to learn that lesson.

We do not generally cancel commitments or change too many plans when we incorporate these young guests into our living pattern. However, we do find ways and do make time to really communicate with them. We want to know where they are spiritually, what they are thinking, and what their goals in life are. The late teens and early twenties is an exciting time of life, but this can also be a perplexing time. It is the time when decisions are made that will affect them for the rest of their lives. These guests can and will discuss their ideas, ideals, and goals with you if you will treat their confidences with respect. Sometimes they will even follow your advice if it is dispensed sparingly with love and great care. Your wise counsel can help make their lives better, and without a doubt their enthusiasm will add zest to your life.

This type of hospitality yields bonuses, one of which is that some of these young people remember us after they have graduated, been discharged, or moved on to other areas. They come back to see us, to introduce their husbands or wives to us, and to let us meet their children. Some of our "early kids" are now making their own homes into "homes away from home" for other grown-up kids. Just as I am grateful to the people who have provided homes away from home for our own children, I have enjoyed the gratitude and friendship of the parents of some of these young people who have adopted us.

If you live in a college town or near a military base, you will find that you have a never ending supply of people who need and appreciate this kind of hospitality. Do not overlook the possibility of making this an international ministry. Every college has foreign students who are lonesome. You home may be just the experience that they need to keep them from despair during a difficult time. You may have to go looking for your first young adult guests, but once the word is out they will come on their own, and people who have not discovered the joy of extending hospitality to these young people themselves will send them to you.

When this happens you will be given opportunities to help these grown-up kids grow spiritually so that they will be profitable servants fit for the Master's use, and you will have a lot of fun in the process.

10

MEET OUR THIRD DAUGHTER

We have three daughters: Anne, whom God gave to us by birth; Beth, who became ours when she married our son; and Chris, whom God set in our family. Each of them is immeasurably dear to us, but only Chris arrived into our family via the hospitality route. I would like to relate this story to you.

I remember the first Sunday she came to church because three of our good, solid, respectable members (all male) asked me if I had met her. She had all the grace, poise, and beauty that could possibly be packed into her small slender frame.

Later that day I learned that she was a dancer who had worked with the Radio City Music Hall Ballet Company. On that first Sunday in our church this young lady yielded her life to Jesus Christ and this, of course, was cause for joy in our home. However I made no more effort to get to know Chris than I would have put forth for any other new convert in our congregation. She was there, a new creature in Christ Jesus, and in this I rejoiced, not having the slightest idea of what God had planned for us.

My next bit of information, as I recall, was that her husband had left her. This is not an uncommon plight for young women in our city. We have a number of them in our church—individuals who have come to us crushed by this type of rejection and have found that there are people who will love them even when their world tumbles down around them.

Next, God had a step of obedience for me to take. It was a
Sunday morning. As I came into the church I saw Chris, and a
thought flashed across my mind. *Why not take her on vacation
with us?* What a crazy idea—after all, we were going to our
favorite vacation spot for a rest.

This spot is an old Victorian house that belongs to one of the
families in our congregation. They graciously make it available
to us each time we want it. It is in the little island town of
Chincoteague on Virginia's Atlantic coast. We love to go there
and walk on the sandy beaches, play in the surf, fish for blue
crabs, and dig for cherry stone clams in the mud flats of Tom's
Cove. But life there is very, very casual—*not the kind of a vacation this cultured, elegant young lady would enjoy,* I reasoned
with myself.

On top of all this, good friends from Texas were coming to
join us, all our children would be there, and there would be no
one Chris's age in this group of people. Where did this far-
fetched idea come from anyway?

It came from God, though I did not think so at the time. Try
as I might, I could not dismiss the thought from my mind that
Sunday morning. I mentioned the idea to my husband that
afternoon and was surprised when Jerry said, "Why not ask her
and let her decide if she would like to go?"

We did, and she came, and under all the culture and elegance
I discovered a lonely girl who needed to be loved and accepted
just as she was—a new baby in God's family. Though there is
a fourteen-year age span between Anne and Chris, with Beth
landing right between them, age seemed to melt away, and that
week a deep friendship began between these three girls. Because
of this friendship, everything from a Sunday dinner to the
Christmas festivities seemed better when Chris was present. In
my thinking Chris had moved into the position of "good friend
of the family."

The telephone rang one night, and it was the emergency room

of one of the Washington hospitals. Chris had been hit by a car. She was not badly hurt but would need to be quiet and to be watched for signs of shock for a day or two. They would not release her from the hospital to go home to her apartment alone, but they would be willing to release her if she came to our house. They asked if we would be willing to assume responsibility for her care.

My emotions were many as I prepared a bed for our coming guest. God took this time to show me just how lonesome being alone in this city can be. He also showed me just how important Chris had become in our lives.

That night after Chris was safely tucked into bed, Jerry and I had a talk. We decided to offer Chris family rights as an adult member of our household. Our married children carry house keys and come and go as they please; we would offer her the same privileges. We did not want to infringe on her independence, but we believed that she needed a belonging place where she could come when she wanted to.

Chris accepted our invitation. In no way did we want to harm her relationship with her own family who lived in a nearby city. Again God's timing was perfect. Unknown to us at this time was the fact that her parents were preparing to move to the West Coast, and they were pleased that their daughter would have a second home.

Imagine my excitement a few weeks later when God showed me just what He was doing by putting Chris in our family. I was reading in the Psalms and certain words seemed to stand out in bold print, "God setteth the solitary in families" (Psalm 68:6, KJV).

That was just what had happened—God had placed Chris in our family. My heart sang as I read and reread those words. They were God's seal of approval upon this new relationship.

Later I wondered if I had missed others whom God had wanted to set in our family. I could have so easily missed this blessing of God if I had hung on to my own vacation plans that first summer. Another question came to my mind: *How many solitary people are lonely because Christian families have not been willing to accept them into their family life?*

Of course this is a two-way street; solitary people have to be willing to be set in families. There is a price to pay to belong to a family. For Chris this price has been relinquishing some of her privacy. She has become a willing resident companion to Anne when Jerry and I have out-of-town trips. She has made herself available to take Anne on special shopping trips, and she readily helps when our hospitality schedule becomes heavy. She lovingly remembers five more birthdays since she has become a part of our household, and she has brought joy and blessing to us that far exceeds any cost in time, energy, or money that we have expended.

Some time ago Chris wrote us a letter, thanking us for her place in our lives. She has granted me the privilege of sharing this letter with you. After reading it I am sure that you will understand how grateful we are to God for setting her in our family.

Easter, 1976

Dearest Pastor, Vivian, and Anne,

Sometimes I wish that you could come into my heart, so that you could really know how much I love you.

When I look to you, I see Christ—His enduring love, His long-suffering nature, His forebearance, His self-denial, His gentleness, His strength, His courage, His humility, His obedience, His faithfulness. All about you is the fragrance of the Savior and witness of the hope we have in Him.

So much of my life was spent trying to escape life, until that night when a dear man told me that Jesus was *alive,* and that He was preparing a place for me in His mansion, and that He loved me just as I was.

All those years, up to that very moment, I had loved and

believed in Jesus, but I had thought He was *dead*. When I was fourteen years old, I cut out a picture of Him and hid it away in a little box, because I treasured it; and whenever I was troubled I would go and take the box from its hiding place; and I would stare at His beautiful face and daydream and wish that I had known Him.

Peace, but then sadness would come over me—I would remember the story my mother told me on that Easter morning when I was seven years old, about how men had crucified Jesus, even though He had done no wrong. (Now, looking back, I realize that it was on that same day, as a little seven-year-old girl, that I became conscious of the reality of evil. I never felt completely safe again, because if men could murder Jesus who was good, perfect in every way, then how much easier it would be for them to murder me, and my brother, and my sister, and my parents.)

I also would remember how my mother explained that the Jews had killed Him because He claimed to be the Son of God, and that they were wrong to do this because He was a great and wonderful prophet; but that I shouldn't blame them because they really didn't know what they were doing.

With those words I believed that Jesus was the Son of God, and I also loathed the men who had killed Him and robbed the world of the Savior. If men could be so blind as not to recognize goodness and innocence, even as they beheld it with their very own eyes then it was clear that "to be good and innocent" was not in itself enough to save one from the forces of evil.

I would wonder if there was a heaven—because if heaven really did exist, then surely Jesus would be there! And if He was there, perhaps I would get to meet Him; and then I could tell Him how much I loved Him. Perhaps my whole family would be together in heaven. (The thought comforted me whenever I thought of my parents' dying.)

But then my father's words would come back to me: "I believe when one dies, that one experiences nothing after that.

There is no heaven or hell—that's something the Catholic Church manufactured to frighten people into leading good lives and to get their money. Why should there be a life after this one? It's the conceit of man that makes him think he has to live forever! As far as I'm concerned, there is one life and after that nothing!"

And so I thought I was being childish and clinging only to a fantasy, just as I had clung to the fantasy of Santa Claus. But then I would read some of the psalms in the pocket-size New Testament that my godparents had given to me. How could the Bible be only a book of myths when it had lasted throughout the centuries? There had to be truth in it, or surely people would not still be reading it and following its teachings? New hope would creep into my heart that God and Jesus and the Bible and heaven were real.

However the education I received at school and at home began to take its toll. The things of the world—intellect, education, prestige, money, and power were extolled; the spiritual things discussed were of man's inhumanity against man. The existentialist theory was expounded as the only rational theory for an "educated man"; therefore it left me with the understanding that insofar as one achieves success (according to the world's standards) one's life is worth the living. And with the converse being only too obvious: those that fail to make their mark in society have no purpose or meaning for living, and their life has basically been a wasted effort.

I became desperate—I wanted my life to count—and the pressure to succeed became unbearable. I began to dread each new day, and soon I began to wish for death, rather than have to face the prospect of failure. I would wander into churches and watch the flickering candles; I would wonder about the meaning of life, and the emptiness in my life only deepened my despair.

The one thing I feared more than anything else was that if I failed, not only would I have lost the one hope I had in myself for success in my life, but, more important, I would have destroyed the belief and hope my mother had in me. And how could she love me, a failure? And I could not face life without her love.

I finally lost the will to live. And in my darkest hour, as I sought to destroy myself, I was not afraid. If there was, as my father said, "nothing" after death, then at least I would no longer suffer. But if Jesus was in heaven, then I wanted to be with Him—I knew He would understand how tired I was and that He would give me peace and rest.

God in His great mercy and faithfulness spared my life, in spite of my sin, and brought me back to accomplish His will. I shall never forget the surprise, nor the disappointment, when I awoke to find myself in my room and not in heaven. I knew God had performed a miracle and that He had a purpose for my life, but I couldn't imagine what it was; and soon I came to believe that it was to punish me for my sin of thinking I could take my life when I pleased in order to come into His presence. So I resigned myself to serving out my time until He called me home.

Six long years dragged by. I passed from one day to the next, not really caring what happened to me. I sought to numb myself and to become oblivious to everything around me, in order not to sense the despair that had driven me to the point of suicide earlier.

In the seventh year, I met my husband-to-be, and we were married after knowing each other twenty-one days! But I felt that God had chosen this man for me, so the shortness of the courtship did not disturb me. I believed that God had spared my life in order that I could spend the rest of my years taking care of Stewart and being a good wife. I rejoiced in having found a reason to live!

One morning, shortly after our second anniversary, my husband sat down and told me he was leaving—he had found someone else.

I felt as if my mind would snap. It was as though I were looking down a huge, black tunnel—at any moment I would be sucked in and torn apart. I remember the incredible calmness and poise I displayed; yet on the inside I felt as if every bone and muscle in my body were dying.

In my anguish, I challenged God to show me that He really existed, that there was a reason to live for Him rather than for the devil.

Pastor, you were His messenger. When you said, "Jesus is *alive,*" my heart leaped up! Joy and hope flooded my soul. I will never forget the wonder of it all—that salvation is a *free* gift, that we need only trust in Jesus, who died for our sins, and rose the third day, and is even now preparing a place for us.

Nor will I ever forget the terrible sorrow, and yet the sweet joy, of knowing that He died for my sake, that I might live. How can such love be possible? And yet we know it is.

I shall always treasure my morning most of all—because I wake up with Jesus! The crushing load of anxiety and fear gone. The darkness gone. To live is joy. In fact, sometimes I have so much joy, that I don't know what to do with it.

No one can ever fully realize the sufferings and the despair or the blessings and the joy of another. But in writing I hope to remind you of the love I hold for each one of you, and why. You cared for my soul then and even now. You have been faithful to me in *all* things—and I cannot say the same of any others, except Christ Jesus. You so gently lead me along God's path, teaching me at my own pace, not becoming annoyed at my "slowness," but waiting patiently as I try to grasp everything before me.

How can I describe the comfort I experienced, even as I was thrown beneath the car, knowing that all of you loved me and would be praying for me and would take care of me without thought to the sacrifice in your time and comfort? If you could come into my heart, then you would know how I cherish each one of you as my own flesh and blood. You changed my life from one of despair into one of joy because you shared the Good News with me; you have given me a sense of worth by showing me that God created me just as I am, and that He has a plan for my life. You have loved me as if I were your own. Think of me when you become discouraged. Remember my smile, my laughter, and the light in my eyes, and continue on for the sake of the one whose soul is in anguish, as mine once was.

I am no longer afraid of this world and its inherent evil nor of the judgment of men.

"For God hath not given us the spirit of fear; but of power, and of love, and of a sound mind" (2 Timothy 1:7, KJV).

"For I am persuaded, that neither death, nor life, nor angels, nor principalities, nor powers, nor things present, nor things to come, nor height, nor depth, nor any other creature, shall be able to separate us from the love of God, which is in Christ Jesus our Lord" (Romans 8:38-39, KJV).

For, "I am crucified with Christ: nevertheless I live; yet not I, but Christ liveth in me: and the life which I now live in the flesh I live by the faith of the Son of God, who loved me, and gave himself for me" (Galatians 2:20, KJV).

Thank you for your loving-kindness.

With peace and joy in Christ,

Your Christine

God has many solitary people who would profit by becoming part of one of His families, and there are families that would find great benefit and joy by the addition of one of these solitary Christians. If this type of hospitality seems good to you, entrust your desire to the Lord and let Him bring it to pass in His time. This is not a relationship to enter into lightly, because good family relationships last a lifetime. God, who knows each of us perfectly, can place just the right person in your family at just the right time, and when God does it, it is very good.

11

SENIOR CITIZENS

In the educational system, to reach the level of senior speaks of achievement. The senior is about to graduate, to complete his course of study, to go on to something bigger and better. It is to be hoped his formal education has helped to prepare him for this new life, a life that should be more profitable and more enjoyable to himself and to others because of his education. He is considered to be a more knowledgeable person because he has achieved the right to be called a senior. It is too bad that most of us do not carry over this same reasoning when we consider the group of people who are now defined as senior citizens.

Just who you consider a senior citizen probably will depend upon your own age. I am sure that some of my young friends look at my gray hair and put me right in the middle of that group. At the other end of the scale one beautiful young lady of eighty told me, "If you write about me, you may call me older, but don't call me old!"

Our economic system "makes" us senior citizens at the age of sixty-five, and our government confirms that decision with social security checks. For our purpose in this chapter we will just say senior citizens are "those people whom you consider to be older." If the young people put me in that class, I will not mind as long as they go on loving me. Here is the real problem of our senior citizens.

"I have come to the conclusion that there is one essential profound underlying problem and it is that the old are unloved.

They do not feel themselves to be loved, and too many people treat them with indifference and seek no contact with them."[1] So wrote Dr. Paul Tournier after studying this group of people for three years.

We have provided our "seniors" with pensions, social security, medicare, and retirement communities, and have forgotten that they are more than bodies that need to be cared for. They are real people who need to have a vital place in our own lives and in the lives of our young people.

Somehow we have been misled in our society to judge a person's value by how much he can produce. When the body makes mass production an impossibility, we treat the "senior" as worthless—just another burden for our society to bear. Unfortunately for the senior citizen and for us, the victim of age often believes us and becomes just that, a passive person who resigns from life before life has chosen to leave him.

These seniors are an open door for the ministry of hospitality. There is nothing that can substitute for love expressed by the "young folks" in the life of an older person (most of us are considered "young folks" by someone).

The Scripture tells us that the person who leaves his own family uncared for is "worse than an unbeliever." Although that text in 1 Timothy 5:8 is referring to monetary needs, I think the apostle Paul would not mind seeing it expanded to include emotional needs as well. If we apply this to the family of God, your church and mine, I am afraid many of us would find ourselves in the category of "worse than an unbeliever."

We gave her a birthday party, and her eyes sparkled with tears—unshed. Tears of happiness? Yes, I am sure that was part of it, but somehow I do not think that was all of it. I knew from the few times I had spent with this charming lady that she had been lonesome between Sundays. Where were we then? Taking care of our own families, minding our own businesses, playing and praying with our own age groups.

Why had she not been included more in our family dinners, in picnics, and in cups of tea and coffee around kitchen tables? It was not because we did not love her; it was not because we did not find her good company; I have to conclude it was because we were busy. Too busy. She concluded the same thing. When she talked to me on the phone she would say, "But I must not keep you. I know you are a very busy girl."

Lord, forgive me for being too busy. Dear friend, forgive me for not including you more when I could have. You have moved now to a place where there are others who are lonesome. Now you are ministering to their lonesomeness, but I wish that I would have ministered to yours more when I could have. Like my little friend Katie, you have taught me what I have missed, and I will try to do better.

Yes, that really happened to me. Maybe something like that has happened to you too. What are we going to do now? Past mistakes are lessons to make the present better.

Are there older people in your church or neighborhood who would enjoy knowing your family better? Even the ones who are surrounded by their own families need us. After all, your own family is required to love you, but when someone else includes you in his life, your sagging sense of personal worth is given an extra lift.

If you have small children, do not overlook the possibility of "adopting" an extra grandparent or two. Little children thrive on love and attention, and busy moms and dads never seem to have enough snuggling and holding time.

In our china closet sit five crystal goblets; a silent, elegant reminder of one of our extra grandmothers. Mrs. Gillespie lived across the alley from us when Jon was born. She was a new widow, seventy years of age, who had had no children of her own. She had never had the responsibility of caring for a baby. Little by little we coaxed her into holding him, loving him, and grandmothering him. Her eyes would sparkle and the lines of sadness would leave her face as she played with him. Gradually they grew to know and love each other. One day when they were having a good time together I slipped off to run an errand, and, behold, we had acquired a babysitting grandmother! Jon does not remember this lady, but someday five crystal goblets will sit in his china closet as a reminder of the love she had for him. Those goblets had been a wedding gift from her husband.

What do you do with older people? Almost anything that they like and that their physical strength will endure. They have not quit living yet. Some of them like to watch football games, and some of them like to play Scrabble. They will all like dinner with your family.

We took one of Anne's favorite "seniors" to our high school production of *Music Man* when Anne had the part of the Irish mother in that play. Joanna loved it. She enjoyed the fact that Anne was in it, and she also enjoyed it ("More than any of you," she informed us) because it reminded her of her high school days. She had clothes like the costumes in that play when she was Anne's age.

Older people like to be listened to. They like to be included in your life. They need to be loved. They are the seniors in the school of life. In our town we see bumper stickers around encouraging us to hug our kids. Have you hugged a grandma or grandpa this week? There are lots of them around just waiting for you.

12

THE PREACHER IS COMING TO OUR HOUSE

When I write this section, I am in home territory. I am married to a preacher, and I have entertained scores of pastors, teachers, evangelists, and missionaries. I find my mind is whirling with thoughts that will need careful sorting; what do I put in, and what do I leave out? Help, Lord!

First I will remind you that these undershepherds of the church are merely men and women. They are the men and women, however, to whom God has entrusted the care of His church. In 1 Timothy 5:17 we are told, "Let the elders who rule well be considered worthy of double honor, especially those who work hard at preaching and teaching." From the context of this passage we know that this has reference to the meeting of the material needs of this group of people. However, I am sure that it can also be applied to meeting the need for friendship and fellowship that is common to all of us. Quite frankly, the ministry would be very difficult for us if the only expression of love that we got from our congregation was a monthly paycheck. We thank the Lord daily for the many ways that our people express their love for us, and we really enjoy being invited into their homes.

When we first began serving the Lord in the pastorate, we decided to accept each invitation that we received unless we had a previous commitment. This sounds like a good policy, but it proved to be devastating. The night that my husband fell sound asleep while sitting on a parishioner's living room couch, we realized that there could be too much of a good thing. As you think of your pastor in relationship to your hospitality, think of his schedule. If you know that he has been out eight nights in a row, but is not committed tonight—well, try to put yourself in his place and do not be offended if he turns down your invitation to dinner—even if you find out later that he spent the night at home playing with his children or reading a book.

I do not know a single pastor who does not enjoy fellowshiping with his people just as often as he is able to, but pastors are human beings. They require rest and quiet times just as you do. Having said that, I am still going to encourage you to invite your pastor over to your house. If he cannot accept your first invitation, try again, and again, and again if necessary to find a time when he and his wife, if he has one (maybe even his children), can come and visit you. This will give you an opportunity to really get to know your pastor and his family. It will also give him a chance to get to know you better.

I think it is much easier to understand and to pray intelligently for people after I have been in their homes. This alone would be reason enough to persist in finding the right time for your pastor to come to your home. Once you have solved this difficulty, the rest of it can be all joy. So, let us do just a little creative thinking on how to find the right time.

To do this bit of thinking I am going to use the life-style of "my" pastor. I realize that your pastor and his schedule are different from that of mine, but I believe the principles of the hunt can work in spite of this. So here is a rough idea of my pastor's schedule.

Day	Morning	Afternoon	Evening
Sunday	9:45 Sunday School 11:00 Worship Service	Coffee Hour (after Church)	6:00 Evening Service
Monday	Pastor's Day Off		7:00 Board Meeting (once or twice a month)
Tuesday	Study Time	Office Work and Counseling	Calling or Com- mittee Meeting
Wednesday	Study Time	Office Work and Counseling	7:30 Prayer Meeting
Thursday	Study Time	Office Work and Counseling	7:30 Calling or Com- mittee Meeting
Friday	Study Time	Office Work and Counseling	Family Night
Saturday	All Those Things that Still Need to Be Done Before Sunday_____		Meditation for Sunday

(P.S. It does not always work the way it is written down. Lest you think this is too much, I will mention that he does try to sneak in a couple of afternoons at home each week between 3:00 and 6:00.)

At first glance, you may think that finding a free spot in this schedule is an impossible task, but it is not. It is a rare week that we do not spend time with some family in our congregation—just fellowshipping, enjoying each other. Remember first of all that schedules are not inflexible. The church services do not move, and it will probably take an "all church" function to change Saturday night. (Experience has taught us that Sunday goes a lot better after a quiet Saturday evening.) Apart from that, everything else wiggles.

So here are some of the ways that we shift the schedule or add to it. One of our favorite times is after the Sunday evening service. This is when this pastor likes to relax and "wind down" with good friends. Sunday noon is all right too, if you can handle it without missing your morning worship service. Now that our children have grown up, we enjoy Friday night invitations. While they were at home we rarely accepted a Friday invitation that did not include them. If the invitation did include them they decided or helped decide if we should accept it. We believe that families need family times, and we found that we did not have them if we did not schedule them.

Sometimes our people help their pastor find time to visit them by inviting a new family for dinner or dessert-and-coffee with him. When this is prearranged, it can fit into a "calling" night. At other times they invite us to come for dinner when they know that there is an evening meeting, understanding full well that the pastor will have to "eat and run." This fact does not keep any of us from enjoying the good fellowship around the dinner table. We also get invited to lunch, and we have accepted and enjoyed breakfast invitations.

When you are searching for a time, do not forget those bonus days, the holidays. For us, Washington's Birthday, Memorial Day, Labor Day, and Veterans Day are not always filled with family traditions. One of the best memories I have from our first year in this pastorate is of a couple calling us on Washing-

ton's Birthday and saying, "It's a holiday. How about letting us
take you to the Red Fox Inn for lunch?" This was our first visit
to this beautiful old inn in Virginia hunt country. The lunch
was just an extra bonus, good as it was. What really made that
day special was the feeling of belonging that it gave the new
pastor and his wife. It was an invitation to share in the play of
our people.

Impromptu Sunday dinner invitations also rate high in
making this pastor and his wife feel loved. Do you know the
kind I mean—where there has been no prior preparation, and
we even are permitted to slip home and pick up our bit to contribute to the meal. It makes no difference if the meal is hot
dogs or steak—it is the being included that counts. For your
sake and your pastor's, do not give up. God gives special blessings to the people and the pastor who find time to fellowship
together.

The date is set—now what do you do? If this is your first
time to entertain the pastor, some of you may be tempted to
panic. Don't. Just remember that pastors are people. Try to
think of what you would enjoy if you were coming to your house.
(A good rule to follow for any guest that you have.) Keep your
food simple unless you get a big thrill out of fancy cooking. If
you really love your pastor, you will not want to contribute too
much to his ever expanding waistline. Think about what you
enjoy doing with other guests that you may have. Most likely
your pastor would enjoy doing that, too. And if you could not
possibly do that with the preacher present, you had better do
some serious thinking about whether you should be doing that
at all.

Do not hide the children. He is their pastor too. I hope your
pastor wants to know your children and enjoy them along with
you for at least part of the time that he is in your home. After
the children get bored with adult company, then what do you
talk about? If your pastor loves God's Word, he will delight in

discussing the things of Scripture that puzzle or thrill you. He will be interested in hearing about your work, your family, your hobbies, or the book you have just read. Do not be afraid of any conversation that is edifying and entertaining. Good pastors usually have a wide range of interests, and I hope for your sake and his—a good sense of humor.

Do not—please do not—turn this time into a gripe session about what you think is wrong with your church or the people that go to your church. If you have such information that you feel you must impart to the pastor, make an appointment and visit him in his office. But do this only after you have prayed (privately) long and hard for God's leading and wisdom.

When we first entered the pastorate, I discovered the amount of work that sometimes lies behind a dinner invitation to a pastor's family. We were invited into a home for Sunday dinner. I was in a bedroom, where I had been instructed to take my coat, when I was joined by one of the small children of the family. This little one informed me that they had worked hard all week to get ready for us. In fact they had washed all the walls because we were coming.

I really hope that you will not find this necessary preparation before you can invite the preacher's family to dinner. I know that I never spend my time inspecting walls or housekeeping in general when I am a guest, and I doubt if other pastors' wives do either. I can assure you that my pastor (and I suspect yours) will never realize or appreciate all your hard work along this line, unless you have a little one who calls it to his attention.

Jesus, when visiting Mary and Martha, gave Martha a guideline for His visits with her. In effect He said, "Martha, don't be so worried about your meal and your house that you don't enjoy My presence here." This is a good guideline for any guest that God allows you to have, including your pastor.

13

THE CIRCUIT RIDER

The circuit rider was the roving pastor of days gone by. He was at one church this week and another the next, ministering to a rather large geographic area. The housing and feeding of the circuit rider was the responsibility of the people to whom he was currently ministering. Today this kind of ministry is not common, but we do still have people who travel from one area to another, ministering in our churches. I firmly believe that the people who are ministered to are responsible for the housing and feeding of our modern-day circuit riders.

This group can include a wide variety of people: the evangelist; the Bible teacher; the leaders of a group or denomination; the public relations people from Christian colleges; musical groups, including college choirs and their leaders; and various other people who travel to promote the teaching of the gospel. Hospitality extended to this group of people often serves to make your family more aware of ministries that reach beyond your own church or community.

These people usually travel on limited budgets, and they do appreciate the opportunity of being your guest. When they come to your house, you may find that their needs and desires are somewhat different from those of your relatives and close friends who have been your houseguests. If your guests are in your town to minister, they will need time alone and a quiet place where they can study and rest before their time of service.

They might like to take a solitary walk to give time for meditation.

Most speakers and musicians that I have known prefer light meals before services and in the case of vocalists, no milk products, please. Many of these same people enjoy rather hardy snacks after their meetings. This is a good time for relaxed fellowship. Be careful not to extend this good time too long, especially if they are scheduled for another big day of ministry or travel tomorrow.

Since the well-being of your guest is your concern, do not hesitate to inquire if he or she is on a medical diet. Some guests will volunteer this information or even send it in advance (which is a good idea), but others will suffer in silence rather than offend their host or hostess. If you have a guest who is on a diet, remember that you do not have to put everyone at the table on your guest's diet. It is important that you are careful to supply some dishes that he can eat without causing him physical distress. Ask as many questions as you need to in order to find out what you must know to meet the special dietary requirements. Then drop the subject, as prolonged discussions may make your guest feel like a nuisance.

If your traveling guest is a year-round traveler who is dependent upon the hospitality of others for many of his meals, I can almost guarantee you that he will not be overly thrilled by the sight of roast beef, ham, or baked chicken. Green beans or peas may not be at the top of his list of favorites either.

If possible ask, "What would you enjoy for dinner? Your choices are ————————." Do not be afraid to include stew, fish, scrambled eggs, hamburgers, spaghetti, or hot dogs on your possibility list. After five days of roast beef dinners, soup and a sandwich can sound like heaven on earth.

Guests who have been away from home for a few days, weeks, or months may need an opportunity to do some shopping, and they will inevitably need to do their laundry. An iron and an ironing board in the guest room, or at least available, may improve your guests' appearance and will certainly add to their feeling of being well cared for.

If you are a member of your church's hospitality committee and have the responsibility of finding housing for ministering guests, do not overlook the fact that a busy denominational executive or a well-known speaker might appreciate the solitude of a well-appointed hotel or motel room—and a loaned car if he uses public transportation. Although these visitors would enjoy visiting in your homes, they often have paperwork that must be accomplished while traveling. Sometimes a hotel room can be the ideal place to get such work done.

Does this seem impossible on your church budget? Then give individuals and groups (Sunday school classes, fellowship groups, etc.) within your church the opportunity to offer hospitality to this guest by subsidizing one night. If you choose this type of hospitality, some meals should still be in the homes of your congregation, and you can arrange with a local restaurant or "room service" for other meals.

Do not leave your guest totally alone, even if you choose this type of hospitality. He is there to minister to your congregation, and he will be able to do a better job of that if he has some opportunity to fellowship with a variety of your people.

The apostle John in his letter to Gaius (3 John) praises him for his ministry to the brethren, especially the strangers. He encourages Gaius to send them out after their ministry in a way that is pleasing to God so "that we may be fellow-workers with the truth" (3 John 8). This is reason enough for me to welcome our twentieth-century circuit riders as my guests.

14

MISSIONARIES ARE REAL PEOPLE

At a denominational conference that I attended, many of the missionaries were wearing lapel buttons that declared, "Missionaries are Real People." It seems we sometimes forget this fact. We become so thrilled with their message of the adventure of carrying the gospel to other countries that we overlook their very human needs.

Of all the houseguests that we entertain (apart from our own family), I would have to say that my favorite group is the missionaries. These people, who have given up the comforts of home to serve the Lord in other lands, are to me a very special group. They came in all shapes and sizes, with all kinds of personalities, and with a great variety of personal burdens—but they have one common denominator. They believed God really meant that we were to "go into all the world" with His message of salvation, and they obeyed.

When they come home they have a story to tell of God's faithfulness in spite of their human frailties, which always have a way of popping up when people are put in hard places. The only way you will ever hear the whole story, and I can promise you it will be a thriller, is by having missionaries as your guests. After all, would you care to tell a stranger how God blessed in spite of your cultural blunder or your anemic faith? Those stories can be shared only with real friends.

The care and feeding of your missionary guest is much the same as that of your pastor or the traveling minister. However, after visiting with many of our missionary guests, I have a few extra suggestions that will make their visit special for them as well as for you.

If your missionaries have just arrived from overseas, remember to allow for "jet lag." Give them time to get their days and nights turned around. This is nice for adults and absolutely necessary for small children if the visit is to be successful.

Be prepared for culture shock. This is inevitable when these people return to our high speed, technologically advanced living. Our life-style is very different from even the city life of the third world nations. If the missionaries have been working in a village or a rural area, the differences become unbelievable.

I like it when missionaries come in family units, but for the missionary this is not always easy or enjoyable. The missionary's child likes the securities of a home just as much as any other child, and he likes his mother's cooking best. When missionary families come to our house, we try to give them some family time alone. I have also been known to give the children a treat and invite their mother to cook a meal.

Missionary parents who have been traveling with their children on extended trips also need some time together alone. Once the children have become comfortable with you, give their mother and dad a treat. Take the children on an outing without their parents. Or send the parents off and plan a day of fun and games for the children at home.

If you are the person in your church who arranges for the hospitality of visiting missionary families, I would urge you to keep your missionary family together as a unit, if at all possible. The temptation to put dad and the boys at one house and mother and the girls at another (or to send each missionary child home with a child of the same age from your congregation) should be avoided. This may sound like a good idea to you, but it does make life difficult for your guests.

One grown-up missionary child told me what this family

division was like for their family. Mother was always concerned that one of the children would get sick in a strange home. Dad worried about the boys' energy (it might be expended in a very "unspiritual way"). Then there was the clothing scramble. There was not room in the car for each person to have his own suitcase, and no matter what combination of packing was used it never was right on the arriving end of things. But of greater magnitude than deportment or sorting clothes was the very alone feeling that engulfed a half-grown boy who was separated from his parents and put in a strange home with strange people. Missionary children will happily sleep on cots or sleeping bags on the living room floor when they know Mom and Dad are under the same roof that they are.

Sometimes you can arrange to leave town for part of the time that a missionary family is visiting you. Privacy is a rare treat for many missionaries on deputation work. One youngster who enjoyed this brand of hospitality declared it was the best visit of the whole trip—almost as good as being home in Hong Kong!

All missionaries have dreams of what they would like to eat when they come home on furlough. Ask them to voice those dreams, and maybe you can make them come true. Some of the things I have found listed most often are fresh potato chips, apples, corn-on-the-cob, hot dogs, watermelon, and pizza. Sometimes this can be reversed. After a few months of furlough, these same missionaries are longing for the ethnic foods of "their country." I have enjoyed asking some of our guests to prepare us a meal as near to authentic as our food sources can make possible. We buy the groceries and are willing helpers in the preparation. We also enjoy some interesting new foods this way.

Missionaries cannot always travel in family units. Often Dad takes to the road, and Mother and children stay behind in a semipermanent location. When this happens you can endear yourself to your lonely guest by treating him to a telephone call home. Learn all you can about his family, for this will give you a better understanding of their life and will help you to pray more effectively for them. It is nice to send a thank-you note to his family after his visit, thanking them for having shared their loved one with you.

Missionary ladies of all ages enjoy an update on current fashions when they come home. A shopping trip for a new outfit can build a fair amount of confidence into a just-home missionary, providing it does not flatten his budget in the process. One of the nicest things a supporting church can do for its returning missionaries is to treat each member of the family to a new in-style outfit as a welcome-home gift.

Missionaries will usually enjoy the opportunity of spending time with the young people of your church. They have a message to give them, and if their work is to continue it is vital that they have a chance to communicate it. You can arrange for informal times with groups or individual young people—opportunities for the young people to ask questions and express their concerns to your visitors. When you do this you may be helping to fulfill the Great Commission. Young people in the company of returned missionaries are shown that God really does go with you and give you blessings that outweigh the burdens when you yield your life to Him for this kind of service.

Those whose lifework is to proclaim the gospel in other lands are indeed worthy of "double honor," and some of that honor comes to them through your hospitality.

15

THE BEREAVED

In our enlightened twentieth century many Americans, including Christians, find it very difficult to deal with death. We prefer to pretend that death cannot happen to us or to the people that we know—but it does. Ever since Eden, the last act of each man upon this earth has been to die. When death comes to the home of a friend or an acquaintance, there is a place for biblical hospitality.

In cities that have major hospital centers there are often people who are all alone immediately after the death of a loved one. Occasionally the Lord has allowed us the privilege of ministering to some of these alone people. They need a place to go until plane reservations can be made. They need some help arranging for the care of the body of the deceased. They need a hand to hold or a shoulder to cry on.

They need to know that someone cares about them. Often they need some simple food to eat, and sometimes they need a mild sedative (the doctor who attended the deceased will usually be willing to supply this if it is needed). If death comes in the evening or night, they will need a bed, and they may want you to sit by that bed for a while. They will need to talk—to tell you how death took their loved one, even if you were there when it happened.

In most cases, listening and holding seem to be the most important ministries that we can give to the bereaved. As they express themselves concerning the loss of the loved one, they are helping their hearts and minds to accept the fact that what has happened is real. When these facts begin to press home in their lives, they need the comfort that can come from human touch. They need to be held in the way that a mother holds a hurt child as they feel those first waves of grief.

Sometimes these people are too reserved to accept this type of holding. Then, just a hand to hang on to can be a lifesaver for them. If it is your hand that they are holding, it is wise to remove any rings that you might have on. Bereaved people hold on very tightly. They have to. A part of their life has just slipped away from them.

Each person's grief is different. There is no right or wrong way to grieve. Do not say, "I understand." Say, "I love you," "I care for you," or, "I'm here to help you." In the beginning of grief it is impossible to believe that anyone can understand. But you can believe that someone can care.

Are you thinking that this is a hard type of hospitality and that you do not want to be involved? If you limit God in that way, I must warn you that you will miss some of the biggest blessings of your life. God has commanded us to bear each other's burdens. When we reach out to the bereaved, God is willing to give us both strength and understanding that goes beyond anything that we can imagine.

One of the privileges of being a pastor's wife is the opportunity of spending time with families that have been visited by death. From that vantage point I can say that what you do is not nearly as important as the fact that you do something. The dinner brought in for the grieving family can be a tremendous help—even when they do not feel like eating it. (Before long there will be someone around who will eat it.) This is your hospitality, brought from your home to theirs.

During grief some adults cannot cope with the children involved. These children also need to be held and listened to. It is better if families can meet each other's needs at these times, but if the adults involved find this impossible at first, you can take the children and be their special friend until their own family is able to take over. This can be an important kind of hospitality. Grieving children have many fears and questions. If you listen carefully you can help to ease their minds. Remember, too, that grieving children still have an abundance of energy that needs to be expended. A long hike or a session with a ball and a bat may be a great release to a child who is trying to cope with grief.

In many cases the extended family will gather for a funeral or a memorial service. Special friends will come from out of town to join the bereaved family. Extra beds may be needed. Do you have one at your house that you can offer? This is hospitality to the bereaved and often, as far as you are concerned, to the stranger.

Some families like to have a meal with close friends after the funeral service. This can be done at the church, but if the group is not too large, it may be nicer to do it at a home. Is your home available for this type of hospitality? If it would not work in your home, are you willing to provide and prepare food to be served at such a meal in another location?

After the burial service, then what? We cannot run away from grief, but it may be wise for the bereaved to go away from the place associated with the grief for a little while. This is often true when there has been a long illness prior to the death of the loved one. Your home may be just the right place for such a person to go. Bereaved people, especially those who will now need to live alone, need someone to talk to. Someone who will listen to the same things over and over. We all need to work out our grief by talking of the lost loved one. True hospitality to these people means listening, listening, and listening some more without becoming impatient.

As we talk about grief it is well to remember that when a person dies, grief is usually a long-term visitor for his loved one.

The time will come when these people will pick up the threads of everyday living and begin to reweave their lives, but the pattern will never be the same as it was before it was interrupted by death.

One lady who was widowed thirty years ago told me that she still dreaded Christmas. She has lived a productive, happy life in the years that have followed the death of her husband, but grief still surfaces at certain times, and loneliness engulfs her. "It really helps to be able to talk to you about it," she told me. She still needed someone who would listen, thirty years later.

In the weeks immediately following a death, many people will "look after" a sorrowing family or person, but what about six months later—or six years later? My heart aches for our widows and widowers who seem to lose a part of their identity in our paired-off society. Sometimes these people remarry before they have time to work through their grief—just because someone offers them the opportunity to escape the loneliness that they have found too heavy to bear alone.

It is not uncommon for bereaved people to pack up and leave the geographic area that they connect with their grief before they know where they want to go or even if they want to go. Often grieving people make tragic financial mistakes because they feel that they have to do something. Sometimes someone will take advantage of them in this time of confusion.

After losing a mate there needs to be a healing period during which the survivor is surrounded by those who care. It is usually better to put off life-changing decisions if possible until this healing process is well underway—at least for a year or two.

Our hospitality extended to these people during this period of their lives can help to keep them from making life-shaking mistakes. If they have a place to go when the loneliness becomes unbearable, they are less likely to move into an unwise marriage. If they know someone cares for them here, they will not be as liable to try to run away. If you are willing to listen, you may be able to give a word of advice that will keep them from financial errors.

The day will come when your bereaved friend's life will again come into focus, and if you have been there with an open door and a listening ear during the healing time, you will be able to share the joy that comes after the night of weeping. Hospitality to the bereaved will give you a true understanding of the phrase "underneath are the everlasting arms" (Deuteronomy 33:27), for you will have seen the holding power of the love of God, even in the face of death. Then you will be able to shout with the apostle Paul, "DEATH IS SWALLOWED UP IN VICTORY. O DEATH, WHERE IS YOUR VICTORY? O DEATH, WHERE IS YOUR STING? The sting of death is sin and the power of sin is the law; but thanks be to God, who gives us the victory through our Lord Jesus Christ" (1 Corinthians 15:54b-57).

16

NO VACANCY

There are creatures and people in this world that God does not intend for us to entertain. Sometimes we become so concerned with being nice that we entertain those whom we should not. This happens when we are not aware of some of God's commandments, or when we choose not to be directed by God's commandments. It happened first in Eden.

Eve was apparently looking at the tree of which God had forbidden Adam (and Eve) to eat. Eve knew God's command concerning that tree. I suspect that Eve knew God's command to Adam to dress and keep Eden, and I am sure that God had informed her that her task was to help Adam as he cared for their beautiful home. I also think that Eve may not have been about her God-given tasks when Satan came to call. At least if she was, we know that she took time out to visit. The horrible consequences of that visit are biblical history. Eve entertained the wrong creature, and the whole pattern of her life was changed forever.

An old proverb says, "The devil tempts every man, but an idle man tempts the devil." When we are neglecting the things that God commands us to do, we are much more liable to find ourselves keeping company with our adversary.

Just as God's servants come to us in the form of human beings, so do Satan's. If we are not being led by the Holy Spirit, we may find ourselves entertaining Satan's messengers. These messengers may even be those who are known to be disciples—

remember when Jesus rebuked Peter by saying, "Get thee behind me, Satan"? This did not mean that Jesus was rejecting Peter, but rather that Peter was at that moment allowing Satan to promote a plan that was in opposition to God's plan.

1 Corinthians 5:11 says, "But actually, I wrote to you not to associate with any so-called brother if he should be an immoral person, or covetous, or an idolater, or a reviler, or a drunkard, or a swindler—not even to eat with such a one." Notice that this verse is dealing with professing Christians. It does not excuse us from working with non-Christians who live in these sins. But when Christians fall into this type of life-style, we are to attempt to restore them to fellowship. If these efforts are not successful, we are to let them alone.

Very often churches are divided because well-meaning Christians attempt to do more than God commands. They try to make these people feel that they are important to them by inviting them to dinner and listening to the accounts of how they feel and how they are being mistreated by their church. The biblical command is clear—if they refuse to repent of their sin, let them alone. People who are used to spiritual fellowship—even those now living in rebellion—miss it if they do not have it. This leaving-alone action can bring a rebellious Christian to repentance. When we do not withhold our hospitality from these people, we are actually helping them to remain in a state of rebellion.

We are not to entertain the freeloader, the lazy man. Paul told the Christians at Thessalonica that if a person would not get busy and do his share of work, they were not to feed him. We are to encourage such a man to find work, help him acquire skills that will enable him to find a job, but not to support him if he is lazy. Hunger is a great motivator. If we set a place at our table for the lazy person, we are destroying the very motivation that God built into him to send him to work.

By the way, Mom and Dad, this is also very usable with your

children. When they decide not to do the reasonable tasks that you assign to them, get out your Bible and read to them the passage in 2 Thessalonians 3:6-10. Use one of the good new translations or paraphrases so that they will be sure to understand God's message. Inform them that if they want a place at the dinner table tonight, they must get busy. After all, you are committed to obeying God's Word and on this point God's Word speaks clearly. You will be equipping your child to receive God's blessing in life as you teach God's principles for living. God blesses obedience.

There is one other type of person that we are not to invite into our homes. In 2 John, verses 7-11 (NIV*), we are told not to entertain those who run ahead and do not continue in the teachings of Christ. This is the deceiver, the false teacher, the heretic who, by either his speech or his life-style, denies the message of Jesus Christ. Often these people are easily discerned, but sometimes they manage to deceive us if we allow ourselves to become too busy or too preoccupied to find out what God wants from us. When this happens, Satan tricks us into participating in the wicked work of these people.

The most rude houseguest that I ever entertained was a preacher who fell into this category. He was sent to us by an organization that is dedicated to serving God. (He fooled them, too!) His spoken message was without a flaw. As he was in our home and as I listened to him preach in our church, I wondered why I was so uncomfortable about this man.

"Lord," I pleaded, "he is serving you, why don't you let me enjoy him?"

A month or so later I received my answer. A Christian from another area told me that though this preacher said the right words, he was deliberately living in direct disobedience to God's commandments. He was a deceiver. We had accepted the recommendation of a well-meaning committee of Christians with-

New International Version.

out checking out our invited guest with people who knew him personally or with the Lord. We had been deceived, and there was no way that God could bless that act of hospitality. We had helped an evil work.

As we use our homes as places to serve God, we must be careful not to misuse them. God's commandments are clear. There are times when we must put up No Vacancy signs if we want God's blessing. Read the following warning Scriptures to know God's commands, and rely on the Holy Spirit to give you right judgment when questions arise.

I wrote you in my letter not to associate with immoral people; I did not at all mean with the immoral people of this world, or with the covetous and swindlers, or with idolaters; for then you would have to go out of the world. But actually, I wrote to you not to associate with any so-called brother if he should be an immoral person, or covetous, or an idolator, or a reviler, or a drunkard, or a swindler—not even to eat with such a one (1 Corinthians 5:9-11).

Now we command you, brethren, in the name of our Lord Jesus Christ, that you keep aloof from every brother who leads an unruly life and not according to the tradition which you received from us. For you yourselves know how you ought to follow our example, because we did not act in an undisciplined manner among you, nor did we eat anyone's bread without paying for it, but with labor and hardship we kept working night and day so that we might not be a burden to any of you; not because we do not have the right to this, but in order to offer ourselves as a model for you, that you might follow our example. For even when we were with you, we used to give you this order: If anyone will not work, neither let him eat (2 Thessalonians 3:6-10).

Watch yourselves, that you might not lose what we have accomplished, but that you may receive a full reward. Any one who goes too far and does not abide in the teaching of Christ, does not have God; the one who abides in the teachıng, he has both the Father and the Son. If any one comes to you and does not bring this teaching, do not receive him into your house, and do not give him a greeting; for the one who gives him a greeting participates in his evil deeds (2 John 8-11).

Part Three

THE WAYS AND MEANS
DEPARTMENT

Commit your works to the Lord,
And your plans will be established.

PROVERBS 16:3

17

KEEP IT SIMPLE

In our fast moving society we all need a retreat, a place where the complications of life seem to melt away, a place where we are accepted, a place where we can simply be our imperfect selves. This is the type of refuge our Christian homes should be for our families and for the guests that God sends to us.

Simplicity in living begins with honesty. Do not try to be something or someone different when you have company than you are when you are alone. This is easier to do when you take the time and effort to realize that God is your Creator. When God creates, it is good. So why not let your guests really enjoy God's creation—you—just as you are.

If you feel that you must put on a special front for company, you had better examine your home-front personality. After all, the members of your own family are the most important people in your life, and they deserve the very best of you. Our children and our mates need to be comfortably sure of how we will react to a given situation whether we are alone or have guests. Life is much simpler when you do not have to second-guess the people you love the most.

Our guests will be more relaxed and at home if they see the real us rather than an overly nice version that will probably crack a bit before the visit is over and make everyone uncomfortable. If you remember that your guests are people who get tired and hungry, who have joys to share and sorrows to bear, and who desire fellowship sometimes and solitude at other times (just as you do), it is not too hard to understand that when you lovingly minister to these needs they will enjoy their visit with you.

My real freedom in hospitality came when I quit cleaning house for company and started keeping house according to a standard that was acceptable to my family. This did not mean that I stopped cleaning, straightening, or thinking of ways to make our home more attractive. I am sure that God puts no premium on dirt, disorder, or jarring color combinations. It did mean that we decided what made living most enjoyable for our own family. It also meant that we had to decide how much time and energy we were willing to devote to the home maintenance department of living.

We came to the conclusion that our home was not a museum, but rather a laboratory for living. It is the place where we do the things that we enjoy, experiment with new ideas and projects, and it is where we look for better solutions to life's problems.

This meant that any dream I held of that model-home look had to go. You have seen that type of home; you walk through and look and admire, but something seems to say, "Please don't touch." We have a number of things in our home that you can walk by and admire, like the paintings our son has done. The canvas, paints, brushes, and paint rags are here, too, in case you would like to give painting a try. There may be homemade cookies in the kitchen, and that may well mean that there is a dirty mixing bowl in the sink. Books, magazines, tapes, and records are everywhere; you are welcome to enjoy them with us.

Our home is filled with possessions that are gifts from God, gifts that are meant to be used, and we will enjoy sharing them with you when you are our guest. We do not feel that all the evidences of living must be removed before we can have company.

Hospitality, to be really effective, needs to be a family project.

If five-year-old Jimmy has to take down the elaborate highway system that he built in his bedroom this afternoon before you feel free to invite Mr. and Mrs. Smith in for dessert and coffee, you can be quite sure that Jimmy will decide that having company is a real nuisance. It may take years for him to change his mind on this subject, too. Why not let Jimmy show your guests his project? Showing is fun, and Jimmy will be learning to like the idea of having company. Many of our guests have joined in with our current interests. Among the many things that they have done is to play instruments, draw pictures, help make bread, and learn to use the wood lathe that lives in the basement.

In hospitality, as in other areas of life, we need to learn to live adventurously within our allotted measure of time, energy, and money. Please do not decide that you cannot have company because the budget will not cover the cost of a seven-course meal this week. Or maybe you have the money for that kind of a meal but are short on the energy or time aspect.

Be creative. Serve something made of hamburger, and do not apologize. Make sure that it is attractive and that it tastes good, and everybody will enjoy it. If you find time is your limited commodity, begin to make it a habit of life to collect every time-saving hospitality idea you can find. Do not miss God's blessing by being too busy. If you are short on energy, look for the easy ways to have company: like dessert and coffee company, or; "Let's have a potluck supper at our house, but please don't bring any desserts. I'll have enough of that for everybody."

God knows all about your limitations, and He has still told you to be "given to hospitality." Two of the most barren years in my life were years when I decided I did not have the time or energy to keep that commandment.

If life is to flow easily within your home you must be adaptable. The more people that you have around, the more adaptable you will need to be. While principles of right and wrong must be held firm and fast, amoral attitudes must be flexible.

When your daughter calls and wants to know if she can bring three of her college friends home with her for the weekend, you will need adaptability and so will she. Mentally you check the bed space, the food supply, and your calendar. The beds are available, the steak that you bought for Sunday can be turned into stroganoff. But, what about that dinner engagement that you have for Saturday night? It really cannot be canceled, so you say, "You are welcome to bring your friends, but Saturday night dinner is cook-your-own hamburger. Dad and I have a dinner date that we need to keep."

The hospitable life can become very complicated if you feel that you must "entertain" houseguests every minute that they are in your home. Our ministry in our own church would suffer if we tried to do this, and so would our family life.

We adapt our hospitality to fit around the other work that God has planned for us to do. We tell our guests what our obligations will be while they are visiting us. Because most of our guests want to sightsee in our beautiful capital city, we equip them with good maps, bus schedules, sometimes a car (if one is available), and any information we might have that would make their excursions more interesting. We also give them house keys so that they can come and go at their convenience. We sometimes invite our guests to fix their lunch or breakfast when our schedules do not match, and on occasion, when we have to keep an evening engagement, we leave dinner ready for them to heat up when they get in.

We even have gone so far as to have houseguests when we were out of town. By stocking our refrigerator and the freezer with easy-to-prepare food, and informing our guests at what address they could pick up a house key, we have been able to share our home with friends when we have had obligations elsewhere.

One of the side benefits of this is the fun of being welcomed home by our guests!

By being adaptable, and inviting our guests to be adaptable, we are able to enjoy many more guests than we would have either the time or energy to entertain in more conventional ways.

Successful hospitality is not putting on a performance. It is delighting in becoming better acquainted with the people whom God sends into your life. It is sharing yourself and your means with these people. It is also accepting them just as they are. If you are to enjoy hospitality you must learn to appreciate people. Each individual that comes into your home is a creation of God. Each one also has a sinful nature: some will have a new redeemed nature as well; some will not. Our task is not to change people. It is to accept them with all their strengths and weaknesses and to give them the life-changing message of redemption in Jesus Christ. God is in the business of remaking each of us from the day of our salvation until He completes the task when we come into His presence. It is our privilege to labor with Him by providing an atmosphere within our homes in which people can respond to His message.

Hospitality becomes complicated only when we choose to make it a "showcase for our abilities" or a competitive struggle to build up our own reputation or position. Hospitality, and life in general, is easier and much more enjoyable when we live by these simple rules:

- Do not have a double standard of living—be consistent and honest.
- Decide on the life-style that is best for your family and live accordingly.
- Live within your means. Finances, time, and energy are limited commodities, so do not overextend yourself in a desire to make a good impression.

- Be adaptable. When necessary do not be afraid to ask others to practice this virtue, too.
- Learn to love and accept people just as they are. This gives God the opportunity to remake them into His image.
- Eliminate competition from your relationship with other people. Seek to gain the approval of God and not that of men.

When you live this way, people will enjoy sharing life with you, and you will be relaxed and able to enjoy the guests God sends to you.

18

CELEBRATIONS

Celebrations are those special times that stand out as the pattern on the fabric of our everyday lives. Here the muted pastels of everyday living are enlivened with the splashes of bright color that come with holidays and other special events. If you think that celebrations are in conflict with the basic theme of this book—which is to share what you have with the persons that God sends at the time that God sends them—just hang on a moment, and I think you will find that they fit in.

Although this is not a book on family living, this section will deal largely with a principle of family living that we believe in. Someone has said, "Success is the journey, not the destination." In our jet age we are all too prone to hop from one point to another and miss the scenery in between. We can go from New York to Los Angeles or from Seattle to Miami and not know anything about the country between those cities. Similarly, in family living, we are too prone to hop from one special event to another without enjoying or sharing the time in between. Most of us will entertain others for Jimmy's first birthday or in celebration of Grandpa and Grandma's fiftieth wedding day. Everyone knows that those are occasions to be celebrated, but we often feel that Thursday night's meatloaf supper is not grand enough to share, so we miss part of the pleasure of the journey. For this reason most of this book emphasizes the giving of our daily lives.

However, every family needs a memory bank of those extra

special good times of celebration. Just as we need to enjoy the journey between cities, we also need to enjoy the city of our destination, if we are to get full benefit of our travels. Much of the joy of family life would be lacking without the special times. God knew this, and He gave Israel detailed instructions for celebrations. We need celebrations to remember. Israel celebrated Passover to remember that God had delivered them from bondage. They have the holiday Purim to remember how Queen Esther risked her life to save God's chosen ones from destruction. As Christians we celebrate Good Friday to remember the price of our salvation, and we celebrate Easter to remember God's victory over sin, which is the basis for our redemption. We need celebrations to remember what God has done for us.

All special days are not directly connected to our spiritual heritage, but all celebrations within the Christian home should reflect a spiritual emphasis. Romans 14:6 tells us that he who regards one day as special does so to the Lord. Our celebrations need to be God-honoring. This should not be hard to do for it is the "living God, who giveth us richly all things to enjoy" (1 Timothy 6:17, KJV).

If we are not getting spiritual benefit from our special days it may be because we are just letting them happen in a haphazard manner. For birthdays, anniversaries, holidays, and other special occasions, we will need to plan if we are to fill our family memory banks with rich treasures. We will also need to budget. Time, energy, and money will most likely be required in varying degrees if we are to be successful. These times of spiritual importance should not be left to chance, but as we plan we need to remain flexible. We ought to be saying, as we plan our special days, that if it is the Lord's will we will live and do this or that (James 4:15). This gives God plenty of room to change our imperfect planning or to replace it with His own.

Though anyone can plan a special celebration, homemakers usually have more opportunity to do this than anyone else. Too often it is tempting to wait for another time when it will be easier or better. Perfect times are rare. If you are going to act, you will probably have to act at an imperfect time. "Tackle every task that comes along, and if you fear God you can expect his blessing" (Ecclesiastes 7:18, TLB).

When your family has an occasion to celebrate—celebrate to the glory of God. What can you celebrate?

- The beginning of a new year
- An engagement
- A new baby
- A new home
- A new puppy
- Christmas
- Everybody's birthday, including George Washington's
- A promotion
- A wedding
- Valentine's Day
- A football victory (or whatever other sport your family is interested in)
- A new job
- Acceptance at college or graduate school
- The Fourth of July
- The homecoming of a family member
- An anniversary
- Finding a lost kitten
- The return of a prodigal child
- The breaking of a bad habit
- Easter
- The first snowfall
- A bon voyage party
- Coming home from the hospital (this may need to be a low-key party)
- Welcome-to-the-neighborhood party

- An election victory
- A good report card
- Or any other event that you can build a good memory around to help your family and friends remember God's blessing to them.

Celebrations can be elaborate or simple, but they should be different from our everyday life. They need to fit into our lives, and sometimes, to make them fit, we will need to do some carving of our regular schedules. There are times when Mother will have to miss a committee meeting or let the ironing pile up and Dad will have to reschedule an appointment so that they can participate in important events in the lives of their children. There will be times when the children will have to forgo a ball game or change other plans so that they can help celebrate something that is important to their parents or grandparents. This kind of sacrifice says, "You are important to me; I care what happens to you." It builds strong family ties.

Needless to say, all of life cannot be special celebrations. But many of us in our busy twentieth-century living are too prone to overlook special occasions, pleading that we are too busy, too tired, or too poor. Plan, build, and budget for special times. Do not wait until they catch you unprepared. You need to make the event of God's blessing into a time that your family will remember.

How does hospitality fit into all this? God's kind of hospitality is sharing what you have with the person God sends, at the time God sends him. But what if God sends him on the very day you have planned a family celebration? The answer is simple—just invite your guest to celebrate with you. God is trustworthy, even here. He knows that sometimes the family needs to be alone to celebrate, and He knows that some occasions will be even more special because of the presence of the guests that He has sent.

In Deuteronomy 16:13-14 God gave instructions to Israel. "You shall celebrate the Feast of Booths seven days after you have gathered in from your threshing floor and your wine vat; and you shall rejoice in your feast, you and your son and your daughter and your male and female servants and the Levite and the stranger and the orphan and the widow who are in your towns."

This was a feast of Thanksgiving—it was a family time, but it was to include the servants, the spiritual leaders, the stranger in town, and the orphans and widows. This was not optional for Israel; the celebration was to include everyone within the household and was to reach out to others. God commanded this as a pattern for remembering His goodness, and the celebration was to include even those whose life-style was different from that of the Israelites, the strangers within the town.

As we translate this into our lives today we find that we are to include "special" people in many of our family celebrations. Those who are our spiritual ministers may be invited, or those who are new to our area, or those who happen to be visiting from other countries and cultures. The principle includes young career people, students, and servicemen who, for one reason or another, cannot go home to celebrate. It reaches out to those who have no families with whom to celebrate. It means young people, middle-aged people, and old people—just any kind of people of whom God reminds us, people who need a celebration as much as we do.

There are many ways to celebrate holidays and special family days that recur annually. For these times each family needs to build its own family traditions. They need not be complicated, but they do need to be special.

At our house, the person having a birthday chooses the menu for the birthday dinner. And that day is enlivened by the laughter that comes from the comic birthday cards that the rest of the family searches for in the weeks before the dinner. Sometimes these cards are bought well in advance of the anticipated celebration because we all plan ahead for this bit of fun.

As often as possible, our family spends the Fourth of July on Virginia's eastern shore, enjoying the special kind of independence that comes with sand and surf. Because a large house is graciously made available to us, we like to share this week with others who enjoy this part of God's creation.

Christmas is a natural for building tradition into family living. I believe that the rather simple Christmas Eve dinner that is shared with new and old friends, and followed by a Christmas Eve service with our church family, is more important to each of us than the shiny red boots that hang from the mantel or the angel that always perches on top of the Christmas tree (which has to be a live tree). This service is reserved for worshiping Jesus Christ who came to earth that first Christmas Eve. We like to celebrate with the wassail and many ethnic foods that we prepare only at this time of the year.

Thanksgiving is mother's day off at our house. This is a relatively new tradition, and the one that preceded it was equally good.

While our children were small we celebrated Thanksgiving with another family, sometimes at their house, sometimes at ours, but at either house we always included the stranger and those who would otherwise be alone. Together we feasted in California, Texas, Virginia, and Connecticut, always enjoying our visit to each other's home. When this family left Connecticut to go back to California, this tradition came to an end.

We needed a new one, so we made a reservation for dinner at one of the charming old inns of Virginia. Each year we go back to a lovely, southern traditional Thanksgiving dinner, and we invite others who do not have families in the area to join us— Dutch treat. This new tradition has already added many special memories to our family memory bank, and I believe it has created good memories for those who have joined with us in giving thanks to God for His goodness to us.

Along with recurring special days, we also celebrate some "once in a while" and some "once in a lifetime" occasions. A graduation or a new kitten can call for a special family time. We celebrate with a pizza or a picnic, a visit to a special place or a trip to Gifford's Ice Cream Parlor, or any other thing that we can think of to make the occasion special.

Our celebrations have often been enhanced by a heaven-sent expected or unexpected guest. Anne's first birthday was better because Julie was visiting us while her parents were out of town. There was a quiet Easter Sunday dinner that is remembered because our special Mrs. Dee Dee joined us at the last minute. There is a Fourth of July at the beach that stands out in our memory because Chris was with us for the first time. Carl and Alice were there, too—catching crabs with fishing tackle and putting them in paper bags. Jon's birthday dinner the year he finished college has better memories because it was shared with new friends from France.

What am I trying to say? Not that every family celebration needs to be shared with guests, but that when we commit ourselves to hospitality God's way, there will be occasions when God gives us the privilege of sharing some of our good times with some of His friends. Rather than fearing that our happy times will be marred, we should welcome these guests God has sent to help build into our lives some special memories and to help us celebrate to the glory of God.

19

WELCOME TO MY KITCHEN

My present kitchen is long and narrow—not what the kitchen planners would consider ideal, but I love it. As I am writing this book, it is having a face-lift. Little by little, as the schedule of a busy pastor allows, it is getting new husband-built cupboards. I have placed my order with my favorite cupboard builder for leaded glass doors in some of the upper cupboards.

I like that idea, for I consider my kitchen a sanctuary, a place committed to the service of God. I like to fill the room with sweet-smelling savors, but I do try to avoid the burnt offerings! It is here that I cooperate with my heavenly Father in meeting people's needs—for although man does not live by bread alone, he does need some bread and some of the other good things that God created for us to eat.

I have had other kitchens, some smaller and some larger, but their purpose has always been the same—a place to meet the dietary needs of the people God sends to sit at our table. My kitchen is rarely in perfect order, though I aim for basic cleanness. It is a working place, and I have no desire to turn it into a showplace where I would hesitate to leave a dirty bowl in the sink while I stopped to visit with the person God sent just as I put the cake in the oven.

So please come into my kitchen and pour yourself a glass of orange juice. Or, if you would rather, make yourself a cup of coffee. Let us sit down at the kitchen table, where we can watch the birds that feast in the window feeder, and talk about kitchens and the food that is prepared in them.

The Scripture has much to say about food. In Proverbs we are told that it is better to eat bread in a pleasant atmosphere than to have meat in a place where there is strife. My "paraphrase" of that would be, "It's more important to keep your spirit in good shape than to cook gourmet meals."

Kitchens should be cheerful places where good-natured people work. This means that I will need to exercise some self-discipline on those days when I do not feel cheerful. It is possible to act right even when our feelings do not agree. When we do what we are supposed to, very often our feelings will come around to the right spot too. There is no disgrace in serving simple meals as long as they are prepared well. The Scripture seems to encourage it. So on days when your head aches, or maybe it is your heart, put more effort into preparing a "sweet spirit" for your family and guests and let them feast on a casserole or a soup-and-sandwich supper.

Old Testament laws dealing with food were very detailed. God was concerned about the good health of His children. Many of those laws dealt with things that made food safe to eat; they encouraged good nutrition and gave protection from diseases common at that time. Good food well prepared is still honoring to God and a blessing to man who eats it.

Feasts were a part of God's plan for His people. He gave detailed plans as to how these feasts were to be eaten. In some cases, as in the Passover feast, He gave complete menus. The family meal is also important—Psalm 128:3 talks of God's blessing in the form of children at our tables. Jesus Christ did not have a kitchen when He lived on this earth, but He did prepare a meal. In John 21 we have the record of a seaside breakfast of bread and fish that He served to some of His friends. Now I am positive that fish was grilled to perfection and served with dignity.

When God allows us to minister to others at mealtime, our aim should be well-prepared food served with dignity. How can we arrive at the place of being good cooks with the ability to add that special grace that makes mealtime a pleasure? Here are a few suggestions.

If you carry on your business of homemaking in a business-like way, you will find it more enjoyable and will be less likely to fall into Satan's "Poor me, I'm just a housewife" trap.

Equip your kitchen with a planning center—a small desk, if possible, or, at the minimum, a cupboard drawer not too far from your kitchen table. This should be a place where paper, pencils, file cards, cookbooks, recipe files, and appliance service manuals are handy. If it can be arranged, a telephone in this area is nice, too.

Have some good textbooks. Good cookbooks are, or should be, some of a cook's favorite reading material. New and used bookstores are full of them. So save your dimes, put them on your Christmas list, or look for them at garage sales, and don't forget all libraries loan them. Some of my favorites are:

- *Pillsbury Family Cookbook*
- *Culinary Classics and Improvisions* by Michael Fields
- *The Williamsburg Cookbook* from Colonial Williamsburg
- *Creative Cooking in 30 Minutes* by Sylvia Schur
- Any of the *Stillmeadow* cookbooks by Gladys Taber.

If you have not explored the world of cookbooks there is no better time to start than now.

Start a recipe file. I have more to say about that, but it will be said in the next chapter.

Develop a list of basic foods that you use regularly and try to keep a small surplus of the nonperishables on hand. Check this list and your current supply before each shopping trip. In your planning area keep a running shopping list on which you write down the item you just used up.

Plan well your trips to the grocery store, and try to stay out of the markets between your regular shopping times—this saves energy and money. Grocery shopping will be easier and less expensive if you shop right after a meal. How often you need to go shopping is an individual decision. Because I have ample refrigerator, freezer, and storage space, I do one large shopping a month, with weekly trips to get perishables and other items that cannot wait for the monthly trip. This saves me a number of hours each month. I find that it also takes less energy and saves money for I buy in larger quantities. If I need anything in between the weekly trips I will try to get one of the family to pick it up for me. When family members go in for milk, that is all they bring out. I cannot say the same for myself!

Have an emergency stock. This should include the needed ingredients for two or three quick meals that can be served to unexpected guests. Replenish these supplies as soon as possible after they have been used.

Plan your meals. Do not let them just happen. But keep your plans flexible. If the chicken is thawed for dinner when your husband says, "Let's go out to eat," save the chicken for tomorrow even if you have to cook it before you go, or, if you have the right kind of oven, while you are gone.

When I was a new homemaker, I wrote out menus on three-by-five-inch cards and then on each card made notes that helped me improve the menu on a later date. I also put shopping lists on the back of those cards so that I would remember to buy the ingredients that I did not regularly stock.

When preparing a dish that freezes well, cook double. A dinner in the freezer can be a lifesaver on a busy day.

Aim for neatness as you work. But, if messes happen, relax—messes can be cleaned up. I take a great deal of comfort in the fact that one of Dallas's wealthiest matrons once told my husband that if a cook was too neat, she fired her, because the messy ones are better cooks.

When possible, prepare as much of your dinner as is practical when you do your breakfast cleanup. This will help you to be a more relaxed hostess at dinnertime.

Invest in the best kitchen utensils that you can afford. They are the tools of your trade. Notice I said best, not necessarily the most expensive. I personally would not trade one of my old cast-iron frypans for all the new stainless steel ones in town.

Do not clutter up your kitchen with things that you do not use. Pack them away in a box, and if you do not unpack them within a year, give them away or have a garage sale. Do keep out in the open some things that you enjoy looking at and handling. They will make your work more enjoyable. A set of mixing bowls that Beth made me will never see the inside of a cupboard as long as I own them. I like to look at them, I like to handle them, I like to use them, I even like to wash them. They are beautiful in their own right and they remind me of my beautiful daughter-in-law each time I look at them.

Do invest in some pretty, cover-up aprons that do not need ironing, and use them. They are good uniforms, and they save the endless changing of clothes if you happen to have an "in and out" schedule as I do.

Convince yourself that simple, well-prepared meals are acceptable for whoever joins you at mealtime. Remember that Jesus reminded Martha not to be troubled with kitchen details and miss the blessing of fellowship with her guest.

Do have some special meals. This is not a contradiction of the above paragraph even if it looks like it. Meals can be made special by the addition of one or two additional well-prepared simple dishes. Have some dishes that you prepare only on special feast days. These can often be ethnic dishes that are a little more work but that can be made ready ahead of time. When preparing a large feast, have a work plan. The work sheets on cooking for a group of fifty (see Part Four) will give you some ideas of how to do this. A mini-version of these will help you keep your good disposition and make use of any offers to help that come. When involved in a big feast, always allow time for some rest breaks. Ten minutes with a cup of tea (or whatever you choose) in a comfortable chair will do wonders to restore your perspective and your efficiency.

No matter what happens, keep your sense of humor and your good judgment intact. Culinary disasters happen to all of us from time to time. So if necessary, improvise, substitute, laugh at yourself, and go on. Everyone will love you better when they discover you are not perfect. Kitchens have a habit of reflecting the personality of the cook, so why not make yours a happy kitchen?

20

EXPLORE MY RECIPE FILE

When we commit ourselves to a ministry of hospitality, sooner or later most of us end up in the kitchen. The buying, preparing, and serving of food will become part of our work. In this day of high food prices, some people may be kept from obeying God's hospitality commandments. Do not let Satan trap you into disobeying God by whispering, "You can't have company; you can't afford it!"

After twenty-seven years of having company that I could not afford, I can assure you that when God sends company He also provides. Remember that biblical hospitality is sharing what you have with the persons God sends. He knows what is on your pantry shelf, and He also knows all about your budget. You can trust Him to help you stretch what you have to minister to others. He is more than willing to give you wisdom to make your accumulated knowledge work wonders in your kitchen.

But notice, you do need to accumulate some knowledge for God to apply the wisdom to. Part of this knowledge includes a good understanding of nutrition. Money that is spent for food should buy things that will promote good health. This is more important today than ever before because our markets are crowded with things that can be classified only as "junk food." Personally, I do not want to serve this kind of thing to my heaven-sent guests.

Our accumulation of knowledge should also include a working knowledge of what can be done with the food that is in your kitchen in order to make it taste good, look good, and preserve (not destroy) its food value. Your kitchen should become a food laboratory where you experiment to find out what you like best. There will be some failures; this is to be expected. Any scientist will tell you that it often takes more than one try to have a successful experiment.

You will need to collect good recipes (formulas, if you please) to work from. It is never too early or too late to start such a collection. Any child who can read and write can begin, and the adult who has never cooked can start now. This accumulation can and should go on indefinitely—God enjoys variety in food. Look at how many different things He made for us to eat.

I really do not believe that it would be proper use of the talent that God has given to me if I were to settle down into a rut like this:

Sunday—roast beef
Monday—beef hash
Tuesday—liver and onions
Wednesday—something made with hamburger
Thursday—chicken
Friday—fish
Saturday—baked beans.

No matter how well I cook these foods, if they appear every seventh day they will loose their taste appeal. Edith Schaeffer in her book *Hidden Art* says:

> Food should be chosen for nutritive values, of course, but also to give pleasure, and to cheer up people after a hard day's work, to comfort them when they feel down for some reason, to amuse them when things seem a bit dull, or to open up conversation when they feel silent and uncommunicative. It seems to me totally unnecessary for any home, or even institution, to fall into the rut of serving the same thing the same day of each week. One should not be able to say, "Oh, yes, Monday, bread

pudding"—*anywhere*. Meals should be a surprise, and should show imagination.[1]

My own limited accumulation of knowledge has come in a large part from reading recipe books. I go to our public libraries regularly, and I make it a point to bring home one or two cookbooks each time. During coffee breaks I will glance through one of these books. When I find a recipe that interests me I will check to see if I think it meets the following standards:

- It must taste good.
- It must look good.
- It must be simple to prepare.
- It must have only ingredients that are available in our local markets.
- It must be reasonable in price.

If it passes these tests, I will give it a try. Then my family will decide if it will have a place in my regular recipe file.

You can set your own requirements. If you have time to prepare elaborate dishes and enjoy doing so, go ahead. If you find hunting down an exotic ingredient an adventure, go after it. I just happen to prefer staying home to shopping. I would usually rather spend those two extra hours at my desk or in my garden and serve a meal that takes less preparation time.

Besides the borrowed cookbooks, I have a rather large collection of my own. If you live in a city or occasionally visit a city, find a good used bookstore. Most of them have a large selection of cookbooks that can be purchased at a fraction of the original cost.

Do not overlook some of the other good sources of food knowledge that are available to us today. Newspapers and magazines often carry good recipes, along with money- and time-saving food tips. Of course, one of the best sources of good recipes will be your mother's and/or mother-in-law's recipe files, and also those of friends who are willing to share their wealth of ideas.

As you become more proficient in your kitchen, you will want to develop some of your own recipes, "improve" recipes that you find in books, and develop some of your own basic principles to work from. The recipes and ideas that I have included here have come from these latter categories. If they are from a friend I have included the first name of that person in the title of the recipe. The others have come from my accumulated knowledge, or are recipes that I have "improved" so much that they bear very little resemblance to the recipes that I started with. Since I so firmly believe that God likes originality, I would encourage you to go on and "improve" my recipes.

Appetizers start the meal. There are many elaborate appetizers, but I will usually let other people fix them. Frankly, I do not want to spoil the appetites of my dinner guests with these rich tidbits. Usually I use commercial crackers, a variety of cheeses, raw vegetables with dips, and some type of nonalcoholic beverage. In the summer I combine fruit juices with club soda and pour that over crushed ice. In the winter I often use a hot drink. This tomato drink is good with cheese and crackers.

ELEANOR'S HOT TOMATO JUICE

Combine and heat but do not boil:

48 oz. tomato juice
10½ oz. beef broth (2 bouillon cubes in 10½ oz. hot water will work)
1 teaspoon grated onion
1 teaspoon grated horseradish
1 teaspoon Worcestershire sauce
1 or 2 drops Tabasco sauce

This will make fourteen four-ounce servings. If the weather is cold you can be sure that there will be calls for seconds.

Wassail is another favorite at our house. We begin serving it on Thanksgiving Day and quit on New Year's Day, keeping it as a holiday special. I make it in large batches, strain it, and put it back into the juice bottles. Just before guests arrive I reheat the amount that is needed for that occasion. Its aroma is heavenly—as it heats, it makes the whole house smell Christmasy.

WASSAIL

> 1 gallon apple juice
> 1 quart cranberry juice
> 2 teaspoons aromatic bitters
> 2 teaspoons whole allspice
> 1 large orange studded with whole cloves

Cover and simmer over low heat for an hour or two to blend flavors.

There are lots of good dip combinations—this is my favorite:

RUTH'S VEGETABLE DIP

> 1 8-oz package cream cheese
> ½ cup mayonnaise
> 2 teaspoons dill weed
> 2 teaspoons chopped parsley (dry will do)
> 2 teaspoons Beau Monde Spice (made by Spice Islands Seasonings—it is a seasoning salt)
> 2 green onions, tops and all (or, if you do not have them, ½ small onion)

Put everything in the blender except the softened cream cheese. Green onions should be cut in small pieces (1 inch or less). Blend well. Cut cheese in eight parts and add one at a time, blending well after each addition. Chill and serve with raw vegetables.

For variety you can substitute 1 cup sour cream for the cheese and increase the mayonnaise to ¾ cup. This makes a softer dip—good with chips or crackers. Some of my testers tried substituting cottage cheese for cream cheese and reported good results.

This cheese ball is the one we use for open house and almost any other time that we can find an excuse to make it. If wrapped in plastic wrap it will keep in the refrigerator for about three weeks.

OPEN HOUSE CHEESE BALL

Blend in blender:

¼ cup mayonnaise
1 green onion cut in pieces (or ¼ small onion)

Grate 4 oz. club cheese and combine with:

4 oz. cream cheese
1 teaspoon Beau Monte Spice (Spice Island Seasonings)
1 teaspoon dill weed
2 teaspoons parsley flakes
¼ teaspoon garlic salt
1 teaspoon Worcestershire sauce
2 drops Tabasco sauce

Add the mayonnaise mixture to the grated cheese. Chill and form into a ball. Roll in chopped nuts and wrap with plastic wrap until ready to use. *Note:* It helps to dip your hands in cold water before forming the ball.

If for some reason I want a more hearty appetizer than these I will often use this hot clam spread. I was given this recipe by a lady in Pennsylvania, and I would like to give her credit for it but I do not know her name.

HOT CLAM PIE

2 cans minced clams with juice from one can (reserve the remaining liquid and add if mixture seems dry)
1 cup bread dressing mix

Garlic salt to taste
2 tablespoons parsley flakes
1 tablespoon crushed oregano leaves
⅓ cup melted butter
Salt and pepper to taste

Mix all ingredients together, put into a glass pie pan, and
sprinkle with grated Parmesan cheese. Bake at 350° for
15 minutes. Serve with crisp crackers. *Note:* This can be
mixed and frozen. Put it into a cold oven and set tempera-
ture at 350°. Bake for 30 minutes or until bubbly and hot.

Let us have a bowl of *soup*. Soup is good on either a lunch
or dinner menu, and I have a daughter who eats it for breakfast.
If you have a few containers of basic soup stock in the freezer
you can always produce something that will serve as an entrée if
you add a sandwich or a salad. It is also a good first course for
almost any dinner menu. Here are recipes for two basic stocks
and some ideas of how to use them.

BASIC CHICKEN STOCK

A kettle (I use a 12-quart kettle) ¾ full of chicken
parts* (necks, backs, or any other parts you happen
to have)†

2 carrots (washed but not peeled)
1 large onion
3 or 4 celery tops
1 tablespoon peppercorns
1 or 2 bay leaves
2 tablespoons salt
Cold water to cover

Simmer for about 3 hours. Strain and put stock into refrigerator until fat becomes solid. Remove the fat, reheat, and
season to taste. If you need more flavor, add bouillon cubes.
Stock can be frozen and stored until you want to use it.
I freeze it in 2-quart containers, remove it from the contain-

ers, and put it into a plastic bag, just in case I want the containers again before I want the stock.

*The meat from chicken parts after cooking can be added to soups or used in casseroles, sandwiches, or salads.

†I keep a resealable plastic bag in the freezer, and each time I fix a chicken, I put the necks, backs, and wing tips (also breast bones when I bone the breast) in it. When it gets full, I make stock.

Three Uses for Chicken Stock

- Sauté sliced mushrooms, onions, and celery in margarine or butter. Add to stock, simmer to blend flavors. I use about one part raw vegetables to two parts stock.
- Or, put one cup cooked spinach in a blender, add one can cream soup (chicken, celery, or mushroom), undiluted, and blend. Add this to three cups chicken stock. Heat and season with a dash of nutmeg.
- Or, sauté some onions and celery in margarine or butter. Add to chicken stock. Bring to a boil and add some rice or noodles. I like to use the oriental rice noodles in this.

BASIC BEEF STOCK

Make the same as chicken stock except use a large beef knucklebone and some neck bones (or beef shanks if you want more meat). Along with this, put in 2 or 3 chicken backs if you have them.

Beef stock usually looks like it needs a lot of help after you take the fat off. I almost always add a little tomato paste (or some tomato juice) and enough beef bouillon cubes to make it look and taste good.

Three Uses for Beef Stock

- Sauté sliced onions in butter or margarine; add to stock, season with Worcestershire sauce and simmer to blend flavors. Put a slice of toasted French bread in each soup bowl. Add soup, sprinkle with grated Parmesan cheese, and serve at once.

• Bring stock to a boil. Add a quarter cup of barley for each quart of stock. Simmer for 45 minutes and add sautéed sliced mushrooms, carrots, celery, and onions. Simmer until barley and vegetables are done—about fifteen or twenty minutes.

• Chop fine: 1 tablespoon onion, 1 tablespoon green pepper, and 2 tablespoons celery. Sauté in butter or margarine. Add this to 2 cups beef stock and one can tomato soup, and heat. Serve with hot buttered croutons. If you do not have the beef stock, this can be done with bouillon cubes.

If you are out of soup stock, do not despair; just make a good chowder. Because my husband would rather go clamming than eat, we usually have a good supply of chowder clams in our freezer. If you are not fortunate enough to have free clams, the canned ones are just about as good. Or if you do not have or do not like clams, try one of the vegetable chowders. They are all good and all easy to make.

BASIC CHOWDER RECIPE

(If you use this without one of the additions, you have potato soup.)

Sauté 6 slices of bacon and remove from pan (save bacon); if you prefer, you may use salt pork here.

Sauté in the bacon drippings:
    ½ cup chopped onions
    ½ cup chopped celery
    3 cups raw diced potatoes

(I usually start by doing the celery and after a couple of minutes add the onion. Let them get just about transparent, and then add the potatoes for just a minute or two.)

Put the vegetables into a large kettle and add the following:

    1 tablespoon salt
    ¼ teaspoon pepper
    ¼ teaspoon thyme

Use any one of the variations given below:
Add a cup of hot water. Simmer until potatoes are done.
Add the bacon, crumbled, and 2½ quarts of milk. Heat
just to the boiling point (do not boil). Add 4 tablespoons
butter or margarine. Let stand for at least 30 minutes before serving. Reheat if necessary.

Corn Chowder

Decrease potatoes to 1½ cups and add one medium-sized
can of creamed corn.

Fish Chowder

Add cooked, flaked mild white fish (that which you have
left over from dinner the other night).

Vegetable Chowder

Sauté and add 2 cups shredded cabbage, 1 cup sliced carrots, and ¼ cup chopped green pepper.

Clam Chowder

Add liquid from 2 cans minced clams (or about 2½ dozen
large steamed chowder clams that have been minced; this
can be done in the blender with the liquid that comes from
cooking them.) Cook until the potatoes are done and add
the clams along with the bacon.

Build your meal around an *entrée*. Because our schedules are
far from rigid, I like a main course that can rest awhile or one
that can be cooked quickly after everyone is present.

There are also some things that can be partly done ahead of
time. This makes less rush or panic if you suddenly have unexpected guests. In this category I like to have one or two containers of tomato meat sauce in the freezer. This can be turned
into chili, a pasta casserole, or spaghetti sauce. Or a cup of
sour cream can be added just before serving time, and it can be
used as a sauce over buttered noodles. I also like to have some

cooked chicken and chicken stock in my emergency supplies. These will make all kinds of good things, including creamed chicken and biscuits, chicken and dumplings, and a chicken and rice casserole.

The following three entrées will wait well for a limited period of time (20 to 30 minutes). In fact the roast beef and the quiche will both slice better after they have had their rest.

ROAST BEEF

> 5 or 6 pound eye of round beef roast
> 2 teaspoons rosemary
> 2 teaspoons salt
> ½ teaspoon coarse ground black pepper

Preheat your oven to 500°—this takes about 15 minutes. Crush the rosemary and mix with salt and pepper. Wipe roast with a paper towel and then rub with the spices. Place on a rack in the hot oven. After 15 minutes, turn the oven down to 350° and continue roasting for about one hour. Use a meat thermometer to decide when it is done. We like it medium rare. Let rest at least 15 minutes before slicing. I drape it with foil to help keep it warm.

ENCHILADAS

> 12 tortillas (fresh or frozen, thawed, but not canned)
> 1½ pounds lean ground beef
> 2 cups canned tomato sauce
> 1 small can enchilada sauce
> 1 large chopped onion
> 1 cup chopped or sliced black olives
> ¾ pound Monterey Jack cheese, grated (or, if you prefer, American cheese), reserving some of this to sprinkle on top of casserole

Preheat oven to 350°. Brown beef and chopped onion in a little vegetable oil. Remove from heat and mix in chopped olives. In a shallow bowl combine tomato sauce with enough of the enchilada sauce to make it spicy (to your taste). Dip tortillas into the tomato sauce, place $\frac{1}{12}$ of the beef mixture in each tortilla plus some grated cheese, and roll. Place in a greased baking dish. Top with the remaining sauce and grated cheese and bake for 20 to 30 minutes at 350°. Serves 6.

QUICHE

    1 nine-inch pie shell, unbaked (see desserts)
    8 oz. Swiss cheese, grated or cut in strips
    2 tablespoons flour
    1 cup milk
    3 eggs, beaten
    ½ teaspoon salt
    Dash of pepper and of nutmeg

One of the following fillings:

    Sautéed onions and green pepper (1 to 1½ cups)
    Sautéed mushrooms
    ½ pound of fried, crumbled bacon
    1 package cooked and well-drained spinach
    1 cup diced ham
    One can drained crab meat
    (Or maybe you have another idea.)

Bake crust in 350° oven for 5 minutes while you mix the cheese and flour together. Remove crust from oven and spread filling in the bottom, then add the cheese mixture. Combine the rest of the ingredients and pour over cheese. Bake at 400° for 25 to 30 minutes or until inserted knife comes out clean. Let rest 10 or 15 minutes. Slice and serve.

Because I am basically a lazy cook, I like things that can be cooked very quickly. One of these things is what I call a chicken cutlet.

CHICKEN CUTLET

For this you just bone one chicken breast for each serving needed, dip it in a seasoned flour, and sauté quickly in vegetable oil. I use different herbs and spices in the flour for variety. Some that I like are Old Bay Seasoning (usually used on shellfish), or poultry seasoning, or oregano, or savory and a bit of garlic salt. Of course you will want some salt with any of them. With this I like baked rice.

BAKED RICE

¼ cup margarine
1 chopped onion
2 stalks celery, diced
1 cup sliced mushrooms or one small can of mushroom pieces (optional)
1 cup of rice, uncooked

Brown all the above ingredients in the margarine and place in a 2-quart casserole. Dissolve 3 chicken bouillon cubes in 2½ cups boiling water. Pour over rice and bake at 350° covered until liquid is absorbed. 1 to 1½ hours. 6 servings.

For beef dishes use beef bouillon cubes. If you like, you may add soy sauce to your taste to either flavor. If your day is going to be busy, brown your vegetables and rice as you do your breakfast cleanup and set aside until time to bake; then just add the liquid and put it in to bake. If you are not going to be home, almost anyone who is can do that for you, even the next door-neighbor if you are that desperate!

LENORE'S STIR-FRIED BEEF

1½ pounds of round steak sliced very thin (⅛ of an inch or less and 2 inches long—this is easier if meat is partly frozen)
2 medium diced onions
1 pound fresh mushrooms, sliced

In a heavy frying pan (I like cast iron) put:

2 tablespoons oil
¾ teaspoon salt
A sprinkling of pepper
¼ teaspoon garlic salt
3 or 4 slices fresh ginger root, optional (to be removed before serving)

Sauté beef, onions, and mushrooms until meat is brown and add:

1 cup beef bouillon

Cover and cook 10 minutes.

Dissolve 2 tablespoons cornstarch and 2 tablespoons soy sauce in ¼ cup cold water and add to meat. Stir until thickened and clear. Serve over hot rice.

I will sometimes add green pepper and/or celery to this. I also will change the whole character of the dish and use cubed, boned raw chicken in place of beef. With this you will need to use chicken stock or chicken bouillon instead of beef.

As you think of entrées, do not forget to make good use of many of your favorite casseroles that will freeze. I do not consider my freeze stock complete if I do not have a frozen meat loaf ready to bake. Use your favorite recipe and freeze it unbaked in a freezer-to-oven pan. Allow about 2½ hours for baking time if you bake it without thawing it first. Another freezer "must" is Swedish meatballs.

SWEDISH MEATBALLS

2 pounds ground round steak
1 pound pork sausage

Mix these together and set aside:

In a blender, if you have one (otherwise a bowl and an electric beater will do), put:

2 eggs
½ can mushroom soup
⅔ cup bread crumbs (bread dressing mix can be used)
1 medium onion that has been sautéed in butter or margarine
1½ teaspoons salt
Dash pepper
⅛ teaspoon allspice

Blend well and add to meat mixture. Shape into small balls and place on a jelly-roll pan and bake at 300° for about 40 minutes or until done all the way through, no pink showing. This makes about 100 small meatballs.

You can use the remaining ½ can of soup in a gravy if you like, but if you are going to freeze them, do not put gravy on them. Instead, let them drain and cool on paper towels and freeze on trays. Store them in a plastic bag. This way you will be able to remove as many servings as you want at any one time. They can be reheated in the oven in a casserole (this is when you add the gravy), or put them in a pan with just a little water added and heat on top of the stove.

Vegetables give variety—or at least they should. It is very easy to fall into the rut of using the same vegetables, fixed the same way, day after day. God was very creative in the variety of vegetables that He provided, and we can be creative in the ways that we prepare them. Here are a few ideas.

My first idea is to buy yourself a present. Any good kitchen shop now stocks those little collapsible steamers that you set in one of your pans so that you can cook your vegetables without drowning them. This little gadget will improve the texture and flavor of both fresh and frozen vegetables and, as an added bonus, conserve their vitamins. Salt your vegetables, not the water, when you use a steamer.

Green beans—almost everybody likes them, and it is a good

thing. If you are a gardener you will know that they are among the most prolific of the vegetable kingdom. Cook them in your steamer and then add a little butter or margarine and a generous sprinkling of dill weed. The next time you serve them, add seasoning salt (I like Lawry's) instead of the dill. If you are a little more ambitious, cook some sliced celery with your beans in the steamer, about one part celery to two parts beans. Add some toasted almonds along with a little butter or margarine, and serve. Or, if you like, make a cream sauce using 1 tablespoon of shortening, 1 tablespoon of flour, ½ cup chicken bouillon and ½ cup milk; add a dash of nutmeg and pour over the cooked vegetables.

Celery is good raw, but I like it even better cooked. Cook it in chicken bouillon and serve it plain or with a dusting of seasoning salt. Or use the bouillon you cooked it in to make a white sauce (see green beans), and top it with toasted almonds, or, if you like them and can get them, with chestnuts that have been sliced and sautéed in margarine or butter.

Eggplant or *zucchini squash* will make a casserole good enough for a main course. Slice the vegetables and sauté lightly in oil. Layer them in a casserole with your favorite tomato meat sauce (which, if you have done your homework, you will have in the freezer) and grated cheese. I like mozzarella or provolone best. Start with the meat sauce and end with cheese. Bake at 350° until the vegetables are tender. About 20 to 30 minutes.

Spinach is especially good done in the steamer. You may need one of those frozen-food knives to make it fit in, though. When it is cooked, add a little butter or margarine and a sprinkle of nutmeg, or garnish it with a chopped hard-boiled egg if your cholesterol count will allow this luxury. My favorite spinach, however, is creamed with ½ cup white sauce (see green beans) and a touch of nutmeg.

Carrots are something that the children want raw, but even the people who do not like cooked carrots may like these. Just slice them thin and put them in a heavy frying pan with some margarine or butter and a teaspoon or two of water. Cover and cook about two minutes, uncover, stir and cook until hot through but still fairly crisp. Add just a touch of mace or a handful of chopped parsley and serve. Or, if you have a little more time, grate your carrots with a coarse grater, instead of slicing them, and cook them this way. They will cook a little faster and taste like a different vegetable.

Cabbage can be cooked the same way as the carrots but do not add parsley to it. Try adding just a little milk along with your butter and spice. Let the milk get hot, but do not let it boil.

Tomatoes, to my way of thinking, are at their best vine ripened and raw, but for variety try broiling some. Select medium-sized tomatoes and slice them in half. Wrap a partly cooked slice of bacon around each half, securing it with a toothpick. Topping them with a bit of margarine or butter and a sprinkling of some seasoning, basil, or oregano is good. Broil until bacon is done and tomato is hot through. The next time you want broiled tomatoes, skip the bacon and top your tomato with Parmesan cheese and buttered bread crumbs. Broil until toasty. Both of these need careful watching as they have a bad habit of cremating themselves if left alone.

Have you tried stir-frying your vegetables? This is one of the best and fastest ways I know to fix most vegetables. If you have a wok, this is a good way to use it. If you do not, just get out your heaviest frying pan. It will work just as well. Put a little oil in it (the amount depends on how many vegetables you are going to cook, but start with a couple of tablespoons) and a slice or two of fresh garlic or a sprinkling of garlic salt. When the oil begins to smoke remove the garlic, if you use the fresh garlic, and add vegetables. Stir as they cook. When they are done but still crisp add a dash of soy sauce and serve. This usually takes five or six minutes total cooking time, and the vegetables should be cooked just as you are ready to serve your meal. You can use fresh vegetables that have been sliced thin or frozen vegetables that have been parboiled (just enough to heat them through) and well drained. Here are some possible combinations to get you started, then you can add your own as you go along:

Onions, green beans, mushrooms, and a few sliced chestnuts if you can get them (If not, almonds are also good)

Yellow crookneck squash, green and red bell peppers, carrots, celery, and onions

Green beans, sliced cauliflower, carrots, and bell peppers

Corn, onions, bell peppers, and, just before it is done, some diced tomatoes.

I have found that almost any vegetable that can be eaten raw can be stir-fried. Some will cook faster than others—just put things like carrots in the pan a minute or two before you add the other vegetables. If you are combining raw and frozen vegetables, start with the raw ones. If you add tomatoes, do it just before the other vegetables are done and let them just barely heat through. Stir-fried vegetables should still be crisp when done.

Salads can make a special meal—or they can make a meal special. One of the favorite events in our church is the salad luncheon—people bring salads that are served with hot rolls and plenty of coffee and tea. It is indeed a special meal. At our house one of the favorite summer menus is a make-it-yourself chef salad. I fix a large bowl of salad green for each person. Then, in separate dishes I put a variety of things that each can add to make his own salad. These things can include meats, shellfish, cheeses, sliced or diced raw vegetables, always olives— black or green—hard-boiled eggs, nuts, toasty croutons, and two or three dressings. With this we like a loaf of hot French bread, a beverage, and a bowl of sherbet. If your afternoon is busy, all these things can be prepared in the morning.

Any tossed green salad is a winner, and the possibilities are many. Here are a few things that you might try adding to your bowl of *mixed* greens:

Orange or grapefruit segments, along with thin-sliced sweet onions or sliced olives—here stuffed green ones are best—with an oil and vinegar or Italian dressing

Black olives, walnuts, and shredded pickled beets

Sliced raw mushrooms, black olives, and thin-sliced red radishes (a sprinkling of grated Swiss cheese is good here, too).

Another favorite salad is a platter of raw vegetables cut for dipping, with a bowl of dip in the middle of the platter (see appetizers).

Cabbage ranks high on my list of salad ingredients. Here is one favorite. Shred cabbage and salt lightly, add diced green and/or red bell peppers, sliced stuffed green olives, thin slices of celery, and a sprinkle of celery seed if you like. Combine with an oil dressing—I use Good Seasons Italian.

Fresh, frozen, and canned fruits are all important salad ingredients at our house. Each summer I freeze blueberries, strawberries, raspberries, and blackberries if I can get them. They make regular appearances on our table as fruit salads all winter long.

To freeze these berries I just lay them on large trays and set them in the freezer. When they are well frozen, I bag them in small plastic freezer bags.

I also freeze peaches this way, but they take just a little more work. I blanche them, peel them, slice them, and give them a bath in orange juice or pineapple juice (this keeps them from turning color). Then I drain them well, freeze them on trays, and bag them. A by-product of this day's work is a refreshing drink made from the juice that processed the peaches. I combine equal parts of the juice with club soda and pour it over crushed ice. It is a real peachy appetizer that I serve my guests that evening. I have never found anyone who did not want a second glassful.

Here are a few fruit combinations that I like to serve:

Peaches, pineapple (fresh or canned in its own juice), sliced bananas, with a sprinkling of one kind of berry for color

Diced apples, sliced bananas, chopped nuts, mixed with whipped cream and topped with a sprinkle of cinnamon

1 20 oz. can of unsweetened pineapple chunks, 1 can mandarin oranges, 2 bananas, 1 cup coconut, and one cup sour cream—mix together and sprinkle with nutmeg.

Our summer favorites are combinations of berries and melons—watermelon balls combined with fresh blueberries or half a small cantaloupe heaped full of fresh blackberries or raspberries. Or try cubes of honeydew melon with nice, sweet strawberries.

All these vegetable and friut combinations are simple to fix; they are also very good and will enhance any meal; and they are just a few of the possible things that you can try. Now get busy and invent your own combinations.

The recipes for gelatin salads are plentiful and easy to obtain. Here are two of my favorites.

MARGE'S SHRIMP ASPIC

    1 small package lemon gelatin
    1 cup hot water

  Dissolve gelatin in water and add:
    1 cup tomato juice
    1 tablespoon vinegar
    1 teaspoon salt

Refrigerate until partly set and stir in:
1 can small shrimp
¼ cup diced celery
¼ cup sliced green olives
1 teaspoon grated onion

Pour into mold and let set until firm. Serve with mayonnaise.

GINGERALE SALAD

1 small package of lime gelatin
½ cup hot water

Dissolve gelatin in water and add:
1 cup gingerale

Chill until partly set and add:
¼ cup chopped nuts
1 cup sliced peaches
½ cup drained crushed pineapple

Pour into a mold and let set until firm.

Bread is my favorite kind of baking—and it is considered by most people to be an essential part of the daily diet. It can become the star of the meal if it is homemade. The secret of making yeast breads is to keep the yeast lukewarm until it is time to bake the bread. Yeast that becomes hot or cold will not do its work.

If you have never made bread, start with a basic white bread. Work with it enough times to get the "feel of it," and then proceed to some of the other good kinds that you can make. The recipes given here are for two loaves each. If you want to make four (if you have freezer room, do), double all ingredients except the yeast. If the recipe calls for one package of yeast, only use 1½ packages when you double your recipe.

BASIC WHITE BREAD

1 package dry yeast dissolved in ½ cup warm water

Into a large mixing bowl put:
2 tablespoons sugar
2 tablespoons shortening (I use margarine)
1 tablespoon salt
¾ cup boiling water

Stir until sugar and salt are dissolved and add:
⅓ cup powdered milk dissolved in ¾ cups cold water

Make sure that this liquid is now lukewarm (if not, let it stand to cool, or if it is too cold heat it just a little). Add the yeast. Mix in 4 cups white flour, stirring vigorously. Continue to add enough flour to make a stiff dough. This will take about two more cupfuls Turn onto a floured surface (I like a Formica counter) and knead until smooth and satiny. Place in a greased bowl and then turn over so that the top is greased, cover with a clean tea towel and set in a warm place (about 80° to rise). When double in size, knead down for about a minute and repeat the rising process. Divide into two equal portions, shape into loaves, and put into greased bread pans. Cover and let rise until the middle of the loaf is even with the top of the pan. Bake at 375° for 40 to 50 minutes. Remove from pan, butter tops of loaves, and let cool on racks.

OATMEAL BREAD

Dissolve in ½ cup warm water:
1 package yeast
½ teaspoon ground ginger

Into a large bowl put:
1 cup oatmeal (uncooked)
2 cups boiling water
½ cup honey *or* molasses
1 tablespoon salt
3 tablespoons margarine

Stir and let stand until lukewarm, then add the yeast and
2½ cups of flour (either white or whole wheat). Stir vigorously. Continue to add white flour (2 to 3 cups) to make
a stiff dough. Proceed as for white bread, but you need only
to let this rise once before shaping into loaves. Bake at
350° for 50 to 60 minutes.

WHOLE WHEAT BREAD

Dissolve in ¼ cup warm water:
   2 packages yeast
   ½ teaspoon ground cumin (optional)

Into a large bowl put:
   1 tablespoon salt
   ½ cup margarine
   ½ cup honey *or* molasses
   ¼ cup orange juice
   2 cups scalded milk

Let cool to lukewarm and add:
   1 egg and the yeast

Stir in vigorously:
   3 cups white flour

Add wheat flour to make a stiff dough (about 3 cups).
Proceed as for white bread. Bake at 425° for 10 minutes;
then turn the oven to 350° and continue to bake 25 to 30
minutes.

There is another family of breads that many of us who live
south of the Mason-Dixon line consider to be equally as important as the yeast breads. These are the breads that use
baking powder, soda, and buttermilk to make them light. They
are often referred to as *quick breads* because they do not require a rising period before baking. Here are my three all-time
favorites.

BAKING POWDER BISCUITS

Mix together in a large mixing bowl:
  2 cups white flour
  ½ teaspoon salt
  4 teaspoons baking powder
  ½ teaspoon soda

Cut in with pastry blender:
  ½ cup vegetable shortening

Stir in:
  1 cup buttermilk

Mix until flour is absorbed and turn onto a floured counter, knead ½ minute or less, and then pat out with your hands to ½-inch thick. Cut with a round cutter (I like something about 2 inches around—like an empty baking powder can that has had the bottom removed) and place in an ungreased pan. I like mine touching each other as I put them into the pan because then they have nowhere to go but up. Bake at 450° for 12 to 15 minutes.

The less you have to handle biscuit dough the better it is, so as I cut each biscuit I push the scraps back into the edge of the main piece of dough. This way I do not have any leftovers that need rekneading.

BUTTERMILK CORN BREAD

  2 cups corn meal (I like yellow best)
  1 cup white flour
  A teaspoon each of salt, soda, and baking powder
  1 egg
  2 tablespoons cooking oil
  2 cups buttermilk

Mix all ingredients quickly until flour is absorbed into the buttermilk and no more—batter will be lumpy. Pour into an 8-inch square hot greased pan (grease pan and put into

oven a few minutes before putting corn bread into it). Bake
for 20 minutes at 450°.

WHOLE WHEAT MUFFINS

Cream:
¼ cup margarine
½ cup brown sugar

Add:
1 egg
1 cup buttermilk

Mix well and stir in:
1 cup white flour and 1 cup wheat flour, mixed together
1 teaspoon soda

Add *one* of the following goodies: 1 cup chopped nuts,
chopped raw apples, drained crushed pineapple, raisins,
chopped dates, or currants (the currants are my favorite)
Put in greased muffin pans (18 small muffins) and bake
for 15 to 20 minutes at 375°.

Dessert crowns the meal. Personally, I like nothing better
for dessert than a bowl of fresh fruit and a tray of good cheeses.
However, I realize that, at least in our country, I am in the
minority, so here are a few goodies for you to try. If you are a
dessert lover, you will doubtless have more good recipes than
I do.

NANCY'S ITALIAN CREAM CAKE

1 cup margarine	1 cup buttermilk
2 cups sugar	1 teaspoon vanilla
5 egg yolks	3½ oz. Angel Flake coconut
2 cups all-purpose flour	1 cup chopped nuts
1 teaspoon soda	5 stiffly beaten egg whites

Cream margarine and sugar, add egg yolks and beat well,
combine flour and soda and add alternately with buttermilk,

beginning and ending with the flour mixture. Stir in vanilla, coconut, and nuts. Fold in the egg whites. Bake in 3 greased and floured 8-inch round pans for about 25 minutes at 350°. Cool and frost with cream cheese frosting and sprinkle with more chopped nuts.

CREAM CHEESE FROSTING

    8 oz. of cream cheese
    ½ cup softened margarine
    1 tablespoon lemon juice
    1 teaspoon vanilla

Cream together and slowly add:
    1 pound powdered sugar

Beat until smooth. If too thick, thin with a little milk.

CARROT CAKE

1½ cups salad oil	1 teaspoon nutmeg
2½ cups sugar	1 teaspoon cinnamon
4 egg yolks	1 teaspoon ground cloves
⅓ cup hot water (tap water is fine)	1 teaspoon mace
2½ cups all-purpose flour	1½ cups coarsely grated raw carrots
1½ teaspoons baking powder	1 cup chopped nuts
½ teaspoon baking soda	1 cup currants
½ teaspoon salt	4 stiffly beaten egg whites

Cream oil and sugar; add egg yolks one at a time, beating after each addition; beat in hot water; add sifted dry ingredients in about four additions, beating well after each; stir in carrots, currants, and nuts; fold in beaten egg whites. Put in a greased and floured nine-inch tube pan and bake at 350° for 60 to 70 minutes. Cool in pan 10 minutes and remove. This is good without frosting, but if you want frosting try a half recipe of the cream cheese frosting on it or a glaze made of powdered sugar and orange juice.

DATE CAKE

Into a large mixing bowl put 1 cup chopped dates and 1 teaspoon soda. Over this pour 1 cup boiling water. Cool to lukewarm.

In a separate bowl cream:
   1 cup margarine
   1 cup sugar

Beat in:
   2 eggs
Combine date and sugar mixtures and mix well.

Sift together:
   1¾ cups flour
   ½ teaspoon salt
   ¾ teaspoon soda

Combine with the date mixture and pour into a greased 8½-by-11-inch pan.

Combine and sprinkle over cake:
   1 cup chocolate chips (I like the small ones for this)
   ½ cup white sugar
   ½ cup chopped nuts

Bake at 350° for about 35 minutes.

GAYLE'S HOMEMADE ICE CREAM

Beat together until sugar dissolves (about 5 minutes):
   9 eggs
   3 cups sugar
Stir in:
   3 tablespoons vanilla
   1 tablespoon lemon juice
   Dash of salt
   1 quart whipping cream
Pour into a 5-quart ice-cream freezer can and fill to fill line with whole milk. Freeze according to your ice-cream freezer directions.

BETHEL'S CHOCOLATE TOPPING

Sift together:
1 cup white sugar
3 tablespoons cornstarch
3 tablespoons cocoa

Slowly stir in 1 cup boiling water. Bring mixture to a boil and remove from heat—watch it, it can burn.

Stir in:
3 tablespoons butter or margarine
1 teaspoon vanilla

Serve warm.

COLONIAL COOKIES

Cream together:
¾ cup white sugar
¾ cup brown sugar
¾ cup margarine.

Add, beating well:
2 eggs

Sift together and add:
2 cups flour
¾ teaspoon soda
1 teaspoon salt
1 teaspoon mace or nutmeg
1 teaspoon cinnamon

Stir in:
1½ teaspoons vanilla
1 cup currants or chopped raisins

Form into 1-inch balls and bake at 375° for 12 to 15 minutes. You may wish to use chocolate chips instead of currants. If so, omit the mace. Makes 4 dozen medium-sized cookies.

MARGE'S LEMON SQUARES

Mix together:
 ¾ cup margarine or butter
 1½ cups flour
 6 tablespoons powdered sugar

Pat into a 9-by-13-inch pan. Bake at 350° for 10 minutes.

Sift together:
 1½ cups sugar
 3 tablespoons flour

Add:
 3 beaten eggs
 Juice and grated rind of 1½ lemons

Spread over the hot base and bake at 350° for 25 minutes.
Cool and frost thinly with:
 1 cup powdered sugar
 1½ tablespoons butter or margarine
 Juice of ½ lemon

Cut into squares.

MRS. WASHINGTON'S GINGER SQUARES

½ cup margarine	1½ teaspoons nutmeg
½ cup brown sugar	1 teaspoon cream of tartar
½ cup molasses	3 eggs, well beaten
½ cup honey	2 tablespoons grated orange
½ cup apple juice or cider	rind
½ cup warm milk	¼ cup orange juice
3 cups all-purpose flour	1 cup currants
2 tablespoons ginger	1 teaspoon baking soda dis-
1½ teaspoons cinnamon	solved in
1½ teaspoons mace	2 tablespoons warm water

Cream shortening and sugars, add molasses, honey, cider,
and milk; beat well. Sift dry ingredients and add alternately
with beaten eggs; add orange rind, juice, and currants. Then
add soda dissolved in water. Mix well and pour into a jelly-

roll pan (15-by-12-by-1-inch) that has been greased and floured. Bake at 350° until done, 15 to 20 minutes. Cool and frost with a very thin layer of cream cheese frosting or your favorite white butter icing.

This is supposedly an adaptation of a recipe of Mary Ball Washington, mother of President Washington.

MARGARET'S CHERRY TORTE

1¼ cups sugar
1 tablespoon margarine
1 cup flour
1 teaspoon cinnamon
1 teaspoon soda

. Cream margarine and sugar; add sifted dry ingredients and fold in:
1 beaten egg

Fold in:
½ cup chopped nuts
1 can red pie cherries, pitted and well drained (save the juice)

It will look horrible, like something has been left out, but put it into a greased 9-by-13-inch pan (it will barely cover the bottom) and bake it 40 minutes at 350°.

While it is baking, make a sauce as follows:
1 cup cherry juice (add water if you need to)
½ cup sugar
1 tablespoon cornstarch

Mix together in a sauce pan and bring to a boil. Remove from heat and add:
1 tablespoon butter or margarine

The torte can be served warm or cold, but have the sauce warm. Cut torte in squares, add some sauce and a scoop of vanilla ice cream or a little whipped cream. It is elegant and good.

One of my favorite winter desserts is a *hot fruit compote.* This is also good for company breakfast. Put four cups of mixed canned, fresh, or frozen fruit (thawed) in a pretty serving dish. Make a sauce to pour over it using ½ cup melted margarine or butter, 2 tablespoons cornstarch, juice and rind from one lemon, ⅔ cup fruit juice (juice from canned fruit may be used), and sugar to your taste (if your juice is presweetened you may not need any). Bring to a boil and pour over the bowl of fruit. Let stand a few minutes (you may want to carefully stir this) until fruit is warm. Serve with a cream cheese topping.

CREAM CHEESE TOPPING

Mix together:
   8 oz. cream cheese
   ¼ cup orange juice

Whip and fold in:
   ½ cup cream

Sweeten to taste with powdered sugar. Put it in a small pretty bowl and sprinkle the top of it with a little nutmeg. Serve with the fruit compote, hot gingerbread, or hot spice cake.

Almost everybody likes pie. Pie is easy once you learn how to make good *piecrust*—and that is as easy as pie! Here is how.

In a medium-sized mixing bowl put 2 cups flour, 1 teaspoon salt, ⅔ cup vegetable shortening. With a pastry cutter (a little gadget with a half dozen or so U-shaped wires or blades attached to a wooden handle), cut in the shortening until it is the texture of very coarse meal.

Now, here is what the cookbooks never tell you—to make piecrust that is easy to roll, put the whole thing in the refrigerator for about one half hour until very cold (or, if you are in a hurry, try the freezer for a few minutes, but do not let it freeze).

Add ice water a little at a time until the mixture will just stick together (about 5 or 6 tablespoonfuls). Divide in half and roll on a floured board. A pastry cloth or Formica counter works well. This will make enough crust for one double-crust pie or two single-crust pies.

Piecrust is easy if everything is ice-cold. If you need to patch your crust, use that ice water for glue. Just put your finger in the water, run it over the tear, and stick the pastry together. You also seal the edges of a double-crust pie this way. Always remember to put some slits in the top crust to let the steam escape while baking. Unfilled piecrust can be baked at 450° for 10 to 12 minutes. Prick the bottom and sides with a fork before baking to keep it from getting all bubbly.

MY FAVORITE APPLE PIE

Pastry for a 9-inch double piecrust
6 cups pared sliced apples put in the bottom of an unbaked pie shell

Mix together:
¾ cup brown sugar
½ teaspoon cinnamon
½ teaspoon nutmeg or mace
1 teaspoon grated lemon rind (use less if your apples are tart)
2 tablespoons flour

Spread mixture over apples. Cut 2 tablespoons of margarine or butter into 8 or 10 pieces and scatter over sugar mixture. Moisten edge of bottom crust and position top crust (be sure you cut some opening in it for the steam to escape). Crimp edges and bake at 450° for 10 minutes, then at 375° for 40 or 50 more minutes. Serve warm with cheddar cheese wedges.

COCONUT PIE—It is quick, easy, and so good. Rich, too!

    1 unbaked single 9-inch pie shell

Mix together:
    3 beaten eggs
    1½ cups white sugar
    4 teaspoons lemon juice
    1 teaspoon vanilla
    1½ tablespoons flour
    ½ cup melted butter or margarine

Fold in:
    3½ oz. Angel Flake coconut and bake at 350° until set
    (knife will come out clean).

JELLO CREAM PIE

    1 baked pie shell
    1 small package of Jello (you pick the flavor).

Dissolve Jello in ¾ cup boiling water and add ¾ cup fruit juice or the syrup from canned fruit (fruit that will complement Jello flavor). Refrigerate until partly set. Whip 1 cup cream and set aside. Whip the partly set Jello, fold in the whipped cream, and pour into pie shell. Refrigerate until firm, garnish with a complementary fruit and more whipped cream if you like.

If you would rather have frozen pie, use 2 cups partly softened vanilla ice cream (or a flavor that complements your Jello) in place of whipped cream and freeze. You may want to take this out to soften a little while before you serve it—just so it will cut easily with a fork when eaten.

Now we have had dinner. But before I finish this chapter, let me slip in a couple of good breakfast dishes and my favorite pancakes that can be used in some way at any meal.

DONNA'S GERMAN EGG PANCAKE

Melt 3 tablespoons of butter or margarine in a 9-by-12-inch pan.

In a mixing bowl beat:
3 eggs

Add:
½ cup milk
½ teaspoon salt
½ cup flour

Beat with a wire whisk. Batter will be lumpy. Pour into pan with melted butter and bake at 425° for 15 to 20 minutes. Cut into squares and serve with lemon juice and powdered sugar (I just put lemon juice in a small cream pitcher) or with jam. Three servings. If you want more, get out another pan and repeat the process.

EGG SOUFFLE

For each serving use:
1 egg
1 slice white bread
⅓ cup milk
1 slice bacon, fried and crumbled
⅛ teaspoon each paprika and dry mustard

Fry bacon, reserve drippings. Mix eggs, milk, and seasonings. Brush bread with bacon drippings and layer with bacon in a casserole. Pour milk and egg mixture over bread and bake at 350° for about 45 minutes. Serve at once.

THIN PANCAKES

Beat:
2 eggs

Add:
1 cup milk

3 tablespoons melted butter (cool slightly)
1 teaspoon baking powder
½ teaspoon salt
¾ cup flour

Mix well (I do it all in a blender) and fry as follows: I use
a cast-iron griddle, but a heavy frying pan will do. Grease
lightly and heat until it begins to smoke, turn down heat a
little and pour on a little batter (2 or 3 tablespoonfuls).
Pick up the griddle and tilt until batter stops running around
the griddle (if you want really round pancakes, use an
8-inch skillet). Put back on heat, and when the shine is
gone from the pancake, turn it over and lightly brown the
other side. You may have to practice a bit to get tempera-
tures right, but the results are worth it.

I use these pancakes for breakfast, lunch, and dinner as well
as for coffee company. You can use them like a crepe by filling
them with creamed meats or fish (great way to use leftovers)
and serving them as an entrée for dinner. Or you can fill them
with fruit or jam and sprinkle them with powdered sugar and
turn them into dessert. My Swedish friends use lingonberries
here. They can be buttered, rolled, and eaten like a hot bread.
I like them this way for breakfast with sausage and hot fruit
compote. Then—let us not overlook the obvious—my family
likes them with pancake syrup.

This is a smattering of my collection of recipes, which I am
pleased to share with you. I have a big "Thank You" to say to
the ladies in our Tuesday morning Bible class who have kitchen-
tasted this chapter just to make sure I did not leave out some
essential ingredient or instruction. Happy cooking!

21

EXPECT A BLESSING

God wants to bless us. He enjoys increasing our productivity. In Malachi 3:10-12, He invites His children to "prove me now" by being obedient in the matter of tithes and offerings. As we read through the Scriptures, it is not hard to discover that obedience and blessing are tied together.

If you feel the blessing is missing in your hospitality, do not point your finger at your guests. God may be telling you that something is wrong in your own life. Invite Him to show you why you cannot find your blessing.

Selfishness often can be the cause of disobedience. God suggests that I invest a little time in Karen, and I say, "All right, Lord, but not now. I have my own plans for this day. There is another chapter to write, a dress to sew, and I want a couple of hours in the garden." This all sounds good and reasonable to me, but what I am really saying is, "Sorry, Lord, my plans are more important than Yours. I'll take care of me first."

This is pure selfishness. I have ignored the fact that God knows all about chapters, dresses, and gardens. I know from experience that when I put Him first He will take care of these little details in plenty of time. When I choose to act this way, I miss the blessing that God has planned for me. He can find a more willing servant to meet Karen's need, but He cannot give me the blessing that He wanted to because I chose to put me first.

Bitterness is another cause of mixed blessing. God describes this sin as a "root" that travels underground in our subconscious, poisoning our entire lives. This root can begin from a very small seed that is dropped into a crevasse of the mind. A common seed giving rise to this root is the current philosophy "Be careful, don't let anyone take advantage of you." Who said that? Almost everyone except Jesus Christ. He had another philosophy to live by. Listen to it.

> "You have heard that it was said, 'AN EYE FOR AN EYE, AND A TOOTH FOR A TOOTH.' But I say to you, do not resist him who is evil; but whoever slaps you on your right cheek, turn to him the other also. And if any one wants to sue you, and take your shirt, let him have your coat also. And whoever shall force you to go one mile, go with him two. Give to him who asks of you, and do not turn away from him who wants to borrow from you" (Matthew 5:38-42).

"Why, we can't live like that," we exclaim. "We would be completely destroyed. That must be for another dispensation!" Where in the text does Jesus teach that this is for another age? He is telling His followers how to live to bring glory to His name. He is inviting them to grow up and to be conformed to the image of God.

It is possible that as we extend hospitality there will be people who will seem to take advantage of us. But if I am trusting the Lord to monitor my guest list, I can rest in the fact that He allows this, which puzzles me, to happen. He has a purpose for it. Often when I think I am being used, God is preparing me for unbelievable blessing. Here is the story of one of these blessings.

A representative of a Christian organization called one day to say that the group was bringing three people from another country to our city for a week. We are not active in that organization, but the caller wanted us to house and feed their guests. It was not a convenient time to have company; however we agreed to take their guests.

Because of language difficulties there was a mix-up in plans. We expected them to arrive for dinner on the day that the visit began—they came at 11:00 P.M. "Some week this is going to be," Satan whispered, "and after you rearranged your whole schedule to accommodate these guests."

Now that was a seed of bitterness, and it could have taken root and ruined a whole new friendship that God had planned for us. The Lord reminded us of this danger, and we pulled out the seed before our guests arrived.

That week brought untold blessings that are still arriving in our lives some years later. We have three more friends and a new interest in another corner of God's harvest field. Our guests ministered to our congregation and to us while they were with us, and God proved Himself faithful by providing time, energy, finances, and joy equal to the risk. "Lord, if this is being taken advantage of, I'm all for it."

Covetousness is also a blessing-stopper. Have you ever envied another person because of what he had that you did not? I remember once being hit by this with a force equal to a ton of bricks. My husband was in graduate school, and we were living in student housing with "leftover" furniture. This was all right. After all, God's servants count all things as loss for the privilege of knowing and serving Him. The daughter of another one of God's "full-time servants" volunteered to babysit for me, gratis. Now any mother of a two-year-old finds this a blessing, and I was no exception. I went off and enjoyed my day.

When it was over, Satan was waiting to get me, and he succeeded masterfully when I took my baby-sitter home. The home of this girl was one of the most charming houses I have ever seen, but I did not enjoy it that day. My only reaction was, "Lord, how come they get to live here, and I have to live in student housing with that old furniture?" It took a number of weeks before I was willing to either enjoy or share my home again.

God did not give up on me, but I lost blessings because I decided God's gift of student housing was not good enough to share. I needed to learn that God knew what was good for that time of our lives. By the way, some of that furniture is still good, and several pieces are considered collector's items!

We can also lose blessings by *deciding how we will live* instead of letting God direct our lives. Earlier I mentioned two barren years when I decided not to keep God's commandment to be hospitable. We were to have a special service in our church the week I made that decision. We would also have four houseguests, all good friends, and twelve dinner guests on Sunday. I was very tired. The day before our houseguests arrived, I walked up the stairs with an armload of fresh linen and blacked out. Clean soft towels cushioned the fall, and I was not really hurt. Our understanding family doctor took over and decided that whatever the problem was, it was not going to be fatal. Giving me something to prop me up over the busy weekend, he informed me that I was to report in when I told my guests good-bye, so that we could search out the culprit who had knocked me down.

Sometime during that weekend I decided that I was done with entertaining—it just took too much out of me! From now on I would be sensible and not add all that work to my life.

In due time the cause of my tiredness was found. It would be a chronic problem, but one that could be controlled by diet. I was soon feeling better, yet my decision stuck. "Don't bother me with all those people, Lord. I can't handle it anymore." Because of this I missed a lot of blessings, and my relationships with people deteriorated as I pulled my protective shell of poor health around me. This was not because people were not good to me but rather because they were, and I was becoming a stagnant pool of unshared love.

When I finally realized what I was doing, I let down one bar of the gate of my life. For a year or so I extended some hospitality, and I received some blessing. But it was not what it used to be. I finally yielded, pulled down all the bars, opened the gate wide, and rather challenged the Lord with, "All right, Father, let them come, but if I fall over, it's Your problem not mine."

That was the summer of 1976—Bicentennial Year. The Lord took me at my word, and for six weeks we had company every single day and night. And He was more than faithful! He not only held me together, but He also gave me the ability to enjoy each of the guests that He brought. He graciously taught me how to put my guests to work when my own strength was short. He showed me that simple meals were very enjoyable when shared with His friends. He shared his bountiful resources with us so that we could pay the very staggering grocery bill that resulted. Then, when I had learned these lessons in obedience, He stopped the company and gave me time to rest and contemplate the blessing of obeying His hospitality commandments.

In the years that have followed, God has sent many houseguests and dinner guests, along with people who drop in for a few minutes, but He has not repeated the experience of my special bicentennial summer. There is never a week that we do not have some company, and yet, as we have let God do the scheduling, we have found that He balances quiet times and busy times and that He makes sure we have all the resources necessary to do the things that He asks. He gives a peace that can override extra workloads, unexpected expenses, the rearrangement of schedules, and even the occasional thoughtlessness (and sometimes even rudeness) of a "sent" guest.

This peace is necessary if you are to enjoy the ministry of

hospitality. Your awareness of it is directly related to your fellowship with God. No matter how busy the day, make time for God's Word—keep a Bible in the kitchen and snatch a few minutes while a casserole cooks. Invest in tapes of Scripture and play them while you work.

Along with these little spiritual snacks, be sure to find some time each day to go to a favorite "alone place" and have a good visit with your heavenly Father. Remember, "they that wait upon the LORD shall renew their strength." Satan loves to use guests to intrude on your private fellowship with God. Do not let him. Guests are capable of spending a little time (or if necessary a lot of time) by themselves; in fact many welcome these quiet times. Excuse yourself and go find the strength and blessing that come from waiting upon the Lord. If necessary, leave the house to do this. All other blessings for both you and your guests will be better after you have had this private fellowship with your heavenly Father.

Expect a blessing; and, with the hindrances to blessing out of the way, what kind of a blessing will you get? I do not know. God does not deal in duplicate blessings. Each one is tailor-made for the person to whom He wants to give it. He has blessings planned that are just perfect for you. This, however, will not keep me from relating some of the blessings He has given to us. The following is a little part of our blessing list.

- We have good friends all over the world that we have met in our home.
- Our children have had the privilege of having their lives influenced by some of God's very special servants.
- Our church has received firsthand reports of ministries in other parts of our country and around the world, from those who have been our guests.
- People have come to join our congregation because someone they knew had been a guest in our home.

- Our front lawn is smooth and green because some visiting servicemen spread nine loads of fill dirt and then raked and seeded it while they were our guests.
- In our living room, young people have decided to let God choose the course for their lives.
- We have been comforted and encouraged by guests, and we have seen some of God's discouraged children take heart as we have fellowshiped together.
- We have brought old friends together and, as we have listened to them reminisce, we have rejoiced in God's pattern worked out in their lives.
- We have watched new friendships form that have brought glory to our heavenly Father.
- We have had a part in God's tender care of those whom He was preparing to leave this life.
- We have been privileged to share the joys of a new baby just beginning this life.
- There is a beautiful Day Care Center in our church's chapel building because an equally beautiful young woman shared her dream with us at dinner one day.
- And overshadowing all these blessings is the blessing of some having accepted the gift of salvation because they saw God's love expressed by way of hospitality.

Over the years we have had our minds stretched, our lives enriched, and our spiritual vision increased as God has sent His friends into our lives. God has no limitations on the blessings that He will give us when we do what He asks, and that is a blessing.

Part Four

CHURCH HOSPITALITY

Let love of the brethren continue.
Do not neglect to show hospitality to strangers.—

HEBREWS 13:1-2*a*

22

CHAIRMAN OF THE HOSPITALITY COMMITTEE

Dear Abby: I am a 66-year-old man who has been singing professionally since age 7. (My father was a famous singer.) Over the years I have sung and lectured in just about every type of church you can name. This exposure has given me a fairly good education as to what kind of people attend church. But why they attend still puzzles me.

During the 60's, I visited over 300 churches. On my own I conducted a survey, containing one question that could be answered voluntarily (and would be kept confidential): "Why do you attend church?"

To date, of the 195 churches I have visited, I was spoken to only once by someone other than an official "greeter"— and that was to ask me to please move my feet.[1]

—John Charles Thomas Jr., Ph.D.

Ouch! What an indictment on churches. Could this man have been in your church or in mine? I do not think so—and yet there is always the possibility of overlooking the stranger as we visit with our church family. I must admit I have a suspicion that Dr. Thomas may be partly responsible for his aloneness. Proverbs 18:24 tells us that for a person to have friends he must be friendly. But the case of Dr. Thomas is not for us to decide. When a person is a visitor in our church, it is our responsibility to reach out to that person, whether he is friendly or not.

Friendly churches do not just happen—someone, often many people, work hard to create a friendly church where strangers are welcomed in Christian love. When you commit yourself to hospitality "God's way," that may include hospitality within your church as well as within your home.

By now someone is thinking, "OK, lady, but you cannot legislate love." You are right, but you can expose others to it, and love is as easy to catch as chicken pox. If you begin to express love, the kind of love that does the right thing in a nice way, and to express your genuine concern for others, you will be establishing a beautiful pattern for others to follow. As more and more people start to do this within your church, it will become a real feat for a stranger to sneak out of your building without receiving some gesture of Christian love.

It is desirable that the pastors, elders, and other leaders set the example for this kind of love that covers a multitude of sins, gives a good report of others, and extends friendship to each visitor. If you are in a church where your leadership is not doing this, do not despair. It can be started by the quietest, most unassuming member of your congregation. Maybe you are the one whom God wants to set the example. One or two persons committed to biblical hospitality within a church can, with prayer, praise, patience, and perseverance change the personality of a cold, impersonal church to one of a loving, friendly congregation.

I have been greatly impressed by some of the men in our congregation who make it their business to learn the names of all newcomers each Sunday. They call visitors by name on their second visit. This is a little thing, but it says, "Someone here is interested in me—they remembered my name." That is hospitality.

In our city the total population changes by one-third every

year. This means the churches of the area have a constantly changing constituency. It is easy to feel that someone is here only for a year or for six months and to overlook one of God's opportunities. These are the very people who often need the lion's share of loving Christian hospitality. When you are living in temporary quarters, your life is in limbo, and you need an anchor of expressed Christian love from the people with whom you choose to worship.

Although expressed spontaneous Christian love is the best kind to have, we have found that, like spontaneous combustion, it often needs a little heat to get it to explode into action. Here is where the chairman of the hospitality committee comes into focus. This person's tasks are legion and may be shared by many people, but church hospitality seems to work best if one person oversees the work.

If I were to write the job description for the chairman of the hospitality committee, I would begin by saying he or she will be responsible for the establishment of a pattern of loving interaction between members of our church and our guests each time we meet as a congregation. He or she will see that opportunities for Christian fellowship are available to each member of the congregation. He or she will also see that there is opportunity to build bridges of hospitality that will allow non-Christians freedom to walk into our Christian community and to explore God's plan of salvation in an atmosphere of love and acceptance.

From there I would go on to the nitty-gritty efforts that are needed to do this work. These would vary from church to church, but they would probably include some all-church activities and some small group activities. In our present church, the chairman of the hospitality committee is responsible for kitchen management, assigning the use of the kitchen, keeping basic supplies in stock, et cetera. She oversees each all-church social function and, because she is a very gracious person, also helps with many of the small-group functions.

One of the fellowship bridges we have used successfully is the serving of coffee and tea immediately following the Sunday morning worship service. This coffee hour gives our people time to develop firm commitments to one another. It has helped many new people become established more rapidly, as it provides a weekly get-acquainted time.

I think this coffee hour has provided a large part of the "heat" that has established for this congregation the well-earned reputation of being a loving church. During the coffee hour we find out who is in need of special help, and has a blessing that needs to be shared. We discover the new family that needs to be included in small social gatherings and the young mother who needs a few hours of volunteer baby-sitting so that she can keep an appointment. We laugh together, we pray together, and we just enjoy fellowship with the family of God.

Like families, churches need some special times of celebration. These times are to help us remember God's goodness to us and to praise Him for it together. Holiday celebrations are important to us, and our people will work hard to make these times memorable. We also have "Agape (love) Suppers" that are potluck in style. These are held two to four times a year, depending on how full the church calendar is. We do this in place of the regular Sunday evening service. Along with good food and fellowship we have time for singing and testimonies and conclude with a Communion service. These "Agape" celebrations help emphasize that we are one family whose father is God.

Sunday night coffee fellowships also occur with a fair degree of regularity. They are often at the church. Occasionally we divide into groups and go to a number of homes. This differs from our morning coffee hour in that we serve some light refreshments along with the beverages, and the fellowship time is somewhat longer.

Our men meet biweekly for study and fellowship on Saturday mornings. Here a coffee pot and a plate of doughnuts helps add to the informal fellowship they enjoy. Our ladies do many things to reach out to each other and to their neighbors and friends. Bible studies, brunches, luncheons, suppers, and craft classes all help to say we are interested, we do care. Salad luncheons and soup-and-salad suppers rank among their favorite tools of hospitality.

Yet, in spite of having these group activities, we found there was still a missing element—the one-to-one concern for the individual does not always flow naturally out of group activities. Because of this, our deaconesses have divided the congregation into nine groups. Each of these ladies oversees the needs of her group. She is committed to a personal contact with each family in her group each month. The contact may be as simple as a phone call or it can be to arrange for something like the care of the children if the mother has a visit to the hospital.

Along with all these planned activities, individuals express love to each other and to the visitors in dozens of little ways each week. Added together, this makes a family atmosphere that always has room for the guest that God chooses to send to us.

To help meet the needs of these guests, our lovely church kitchen has become a busy place. We believe that presenting Christ is often easier, and that many people are more receptive, when we serve physical food along with spiritual truth. Many of our ladies—and our men—have cooked there for the glory of God. This is part of our spiritual work. Here, as in your own kitchen, accumulated knowledge applied along with God-given wisdom is invaluable.

If you have never cooked for a large group there is no better time than now to start. The same basic principle of good food simply prepared and served with dignity will do the job. There are many good "quantity cookbooks"—my favorite is *Food for Fifty* written by Sina Faye Fowler (New York: Wiley, 1971).

If you are in charge of a meal for a group, you will need to plan well and shop carefully. You will need to find your "helpers" either by asking for volunteers or by approaching individuals. Be sure to tell these people just how much help you want and when you want it. I like to combine the two methods and ask for volunteers for the day before and the morning of the function, then handpick the people who will help when the meal is being served. Because we are all human beings, we need to face the fact that here, as well as in other areas of life, we find some people easier to work with than others. Certain people seem to operate on the same "wavelength." During the busy serving time, things will go more smoothly if your team is made up of people who work easily together.

I must admit that I do enjoy the volunteer system, too. Usually someone will volunteer whom I would never have thought to ask. Working together can bring people into closer friendships. I suspect that many families in our church began to feel like this was really their church when they took their turn in the kitchen.

The better you have planned, the more enjoyable the work will be for everyone involved. When possible, give people a chance to choose the jobs that they would like to do. I have had good success with posted work sheets that list the jobs and the time that each needs to be done. Here you can sign your name after the job you choose and cross it off when you have finished it.

The following work sheet is from a dinner that was done for our Junior High Group and their parents. We served fifty people, and there were seven kitchen helpers—two the day before the dinner, two the day of the dinner, and three who came to serve and do the cleaning up.

MENU

Fruit Punch and Crackers
Breast of Turkey with Gravy
Baked Rice
Green Beans Supreme
Spiced Apple Rings
Jello Salads (variety brought by 6 different individuals)
Buttermilk Rolls and Butter
Ice Cream with Chocolate topping

Punch:

2 large cans apricot nectar	A.M.—Combine all ingredients
2 medium cans frozen orange juice	but soda. Chill.
2 cans frozen lemonade	Before serving add ice and soda.
1 large can pineapple juice	
3 qts. club soda	

Rice:

1½ lb. sausage	A.M.—Sauté sausage and drain.
¾ lb. margarine	(Dispose of fat.) In same pans
6 cups rice	put margarine, rice, and onions,
2 c. chopped onions	and brown. Put into baking pan.
5 small cans mushrooms	
20 chicken bouillon cubes	P.M.—Add the rest of the ingredi-
4¼ qts. boiling water	ents and bake at 350° for 2½
1¼ cups soy sauce	hours.

Rolls:

1¼ cups warm water	A.M.—Mix and shape into rolls.
4 pkg. yeast	Let rise 1 to 1½ hours. Bake at
4½ cups lukewarm buttermilk	400° for 15 to 20 minutes.
1½ tsp. soda	
2 T. sugar	P.M.—Reheat at 350° for about
2 T. salt	10 minutes.
1¼ cups margarine	
15 cups flour (about)	

Green Beans:

6 cups sliced celery	A.M.—Slice celery and sauté in margarine. Cook beans in salt water until barely tender. Drain.
1½ cups margarine	
Green beans (about 8 lbs. frozen)	
Toasted almonds (1 pound sliced)	P.M.—Combine, heat thoroughly, and season to taste.
Seasoning salt	

Chocolate Topping:

5 cups sugar	A.M.—In saucepan or double boiler combine sugar, cornstarch, and cocoa, working until smooth. Add water slowly, stirring until thickened. Remove from heat and add margarine and vanilla.
1 cup cornstarch	
1 cup cocoa	
5 cups boiling water	
1 cup margarine	
2 T. vanilla	
	P.M.—Reheat—*stir* while heating.

Gravy:

6 cans cream of chicken soup	A.M.—Open soup and add water.
3 cans water	P.M.—Add small amount of water to turkey pan and add to soup. Heat and season to taste.
Pan drippings from turkey	
Seasonings	

MORNING WORK

Cooking:

Make rolls
Prepare rice
Prepare green beans
Make chocolate sauce
Mix punch
Make iced-tea base
Begin gravy
Cut apple rings in half
Wash parsley   Slice lemons

Table Setting:

Bud vases filled with water
Placemats
Napkins
Plates, silver (2 spoons), glasses, cups, small dish for jello salad
Salt and pepper
Sugar
Place cards
Line roll baskets with napkins

Set up punch table in hall

AFTERNOON WORK

Cook turkey and rice

EVENING WORK

Finish punch
Put crackers in baskets

Cooking:

Slice turkey.
  Put on platters garnished
  with apple rings and parsley.
Finish beans.
Finish gravy.
Heat rolls.
Garnish salads with Cool Whip
  if it will go with salad.

Make coffee (serve with dessert
only).

Fix pitchers of iced tea and ice
water.

Things to be put on tables before guests are seated:

Lemon for tea
Butter
Cream for coffee
Ice in glasses
Jello salads
Baskets of rolls
Pitchers of ice water and iced tea

Things to be brought to tables after guests are seated:

Platters of turkey
Bowls of rice and green beans

Dessert time:

Ice cream in small plastic bowls (to be dished up at the last minute
  as it melts rather fast)
Bowls of warm ice-cream topping
Thermos pitchers of coffee

Many, many thanks for all your work!!!!!

Jesus Christ established His church upon this earth as a fellowship in which His children could worship Him and enjoy each other. This fellowship is to be a base from which His children reach out to people who are in need of salvation. The work of the church is to edify Christians so that they can do the work of the ministry. We do not want to detract from this main task of the church. The work of hospitality should never replace this task; it should instead be a tool to make the task easier and more effective.

One of the biggest traps Satan has set for Christians who are involved in the hospitality ministry is the competitive spirit. When Christians compete with each other to "set a better table" than someone else, either at church or at home, their work ceases to be a spiritual ministry. It then becomes a tool of Satan to destroy Christian unity within the church.

We need constantly to monitor our motives for service. Here, as in all other areas of our lives, we need to be sure that we are serving the Lord with a pure heart. When we do this, He receives the glory for the work that is done, and we praise Him for allowing us to help. When work is done for the glory of God we do not let the little things (or the big things) that happen hurt our feelings, for we are not seeking praise for ourselves.

I am most grateful for the opportunity to be a part of God's family, to be included in a congregation who have willingly shared with us and have let us share with them in the ministry of hospitality. Together we have learned that God has a marvelous way of multiplying the gifts that He has given us when we return them to Him by ministering to the household of faith and to the guests that He sends our way.

If Dr. Thomas ever has the opportunity to visit your church or ours, I hope that he will be able to discern, without asking, why we attend church. If we are truly committed to the ministry of hospitality, he will find that it will take careful planning on his part to leave our churches without having had to talk to a number of people—people who are really interested in him, not just in his talent. Many church visitors, like this man who wrote of his disappointment in churches, are waiting for someone who is committed to Jesus Christ and who will express that commitment in tangible ways.

Part Five

EXAMPLES FROM SCRIPTURE

> *For whatever was written in earlier times*
> *was written for our instruction, that*
> *through perseverance and the encourage-*
> *ment of the Scriptures we might have hope.*
>
> ROMANS 15:4

23

A WORD OF EXPLANATION

Many years ago, on an evening a few days before Christmas, it was my privilege to sit on the floor of a living room with a group of college students. We were gathered around a chair; possibly it was a wheel chair. This chair was occupied by a lady named Mrs. Dennison. She told us a story—a story that we all knew, but I had never heard it the way she told it. That night the story of the Nativity became alive as this gracious crippled lady wove the threads of culture and history through the warp of the scriptural account of the birth of Christ.

I still remember "Mrs. Dennison's Christmas Story," and each year I look for a group of children with whom to share it. This experience started me on an adventure of study that has lasted thirty years. Whenever there is a Bible story to be told, I want to know the culture and history that can make it a new story for the young people who have possibly known and read the story many times.

As I began to seriously study biblical hospitality I found that God has given many examples of it in the stories of the Scriptures. I followed the path that Mrs. Dennison had shown me, and I began to weave the woof threads of how it might have been for the guests, hosts, and hostesses of Scripture through the warp threads of the various texts. Almost immediately, patterns began to show up that illustrated the biblical commands for hospitality. These were patterns that I could follow as I extended hospitality to those whom God chose to be my guests. Because the biblical stories teach these truths so beautifully to both children and adults I want to relate a few of them in this book.

I have tried to work carefully for I believe it is important not to misrepresent the facts in the stories of the Bible. I have tried to distinguish clearly the "what might have happened" parts from the "what did happen" parts of the stories.

When God commanded hospitality, He made sure He supplied us with an adequate number of Bible stories that illustrate hospitality. It has been hard to decide which examples to include in this part of this book. I have picked eight, most of them not usually connected with lessons on hospitality. I invite you to be my guest, to enjoy them and learn from them, even as I have.

24

WELCOME TO EDEN

Two Scriptures that send my imagination soaring are found in Genesis 2:8 and 2:15. They simply say, "And the LORD God planted a garden eastward in Eden; and there he put the man whom he had formed. . . . And the LORD God took the man, and put him into the garden of Eden to dress it and to keep it" (KJV).

The six intervening verses give us the only description of Adam's first home. Any gardener can enjoy the description of this well-planted garden among rivers whose beaches were decorated with nuggets of gold having shiny black onyx for contrast. This garden had trees of infinite variety, all beautiful to look at, and some of them bore fruit that would delight the gourmet. But this is not a garden book, so why take a path into Eden?

Eden was the first home on this earth. What a beautiful place for hospitality to begin! Adam was Eden's resident keeper. God put him there—gave him a lease, if you please. This lease carried with it certain obligations.

After God put Adam in his new home, He stayed on to see that he got settled in this home. I like to think that God was Adam's first guest. Can you imagine what kind of fellowship there could have been? As God observed Adam in his garden home, He must have sensed a restlessness in this person who was made in His image. He said, "It is not good that the man should be alone" (Genesis 2:18, KJV).

Fluffy, furry cats were entertaining, monkeys using the beautiful trees for trapeze acts brought humor, the long-necked giraffe could prune the fruit trees, and the graceful birds provided a symphony. But these did not fulfill Adam's need for a companion of his own kind. Just as God desired fellowship with a creature made in "his own image" (Genesis 1:27), so did Adam. I believe that this desire was a part of Adam because he was created in God's image, and God understood. God, who had been there with Adam as he had gone about the business of "organizing Eden" (after all, each of those creatures had to be named), sensed this need. Wonder of wonders, that first Houseguest met the need in the life of the keeper of the home in Eden.

As we delve into the business of practical Christian hospitality it seems almost superfluous to say, "God first," and yet, maybe it is not. Oh, I know all about the wall plaque that reads, "Christ is a Guest in this home. . . . " And in a sense I am sure this is true in the homes of Christians, but just how much do you include God in your plans? Are you aware that God has a master plan for each day of your life? Are you working together with Him?

God and Adam worked together. "God formed every beast of the field, and every fowl of the air; and brought them unto Adam to see what he would call them" (Genesis 2:19, KJV). And what is really amazing about this is that God accepted Adam's work." "Whatsoever Adam called every living creature, that was the name thereof" (KJV). No changes, no criticism— just acceptance of Adam's work. They were in it together.

Christian hospitality only succeeds when we are in it together with God. We must schedule into our days special conferences with our heavenly Colaborer, or our efforts become a useless expenditure of energy. You can trust God. He will not belittle the work you do with Him. He will help get the right person there at the right time for the right kind of hospitality. To work with Him you must communicate with Him regularly.

Though we are not told so, I like to think that God came regularly to walk with Adam in the "cool of the day." (We do know that this was the case on that awful day sin entered Eden.) The cool of the day could be either morning or evening; maybe He came both times.

In the morning it is good to lay a new day before God and say, "Here it is, Lord. Let's plan how we will spend this day to bring You glory." After all, God knows whether the missionary who is arriving today is dead tired and would find the most hospitable treatment to be provided a simple family dinner and an early bedtime, or if he is just bubbling over with what is happening in his place of service and would like nothing better than to find around your dinner table two or three interested couples with whom to share God's blessings. God has access to this kind of knowledge, which can make you the gracious, sensitive host or hostess He wants you to be. It is important to take the time to find out from God just how your ministry of hospitality can be most useful.

Remember that God sensed Adam's need. He knows yours, too, and He wants to meet it. One thing is necessary if He is to meet our needs. We must trust Him totally. Sometimes the guest that comes at the most inopportune time (by our standards) is just the one God is planning to use to meet our need. We will be the loser if we say, "Not today, God," and give our human excuses.

God also knows when to cancel out a planned guest. Have you ever cooked a company meal and completed all the necessary arrangements only to have your guests call and cancel? Or maybe they did not even call. Humanly speaking, that is hard to take. But if God is in charge, you can be sure that it is right, and you can draw upon His grace to remain in good humor, without malice toward your invited guests. What a fine time to have a family party and really enjoy each other without the responsibility of company! Or maybe this is the right way to get to know the new people who just moved in next door. Tell them what happened and ask them to help you out by being your company tonight.

Talk over your plans with God in the cool of the morning. Give Him the freedom to change them, add to them, cancel them, or anything else He desires. If God puts a certain name in your mind, explore with Him just what would be the best action for you to take. Sometimes the answer will be to pray, sometimes it will be to act. Whatever the answer, we need to be willing to conform to God's higher wisdom.

The cool of evening is another good time to commune with God. Now we can review the day, commit the work that has been done to Him, thank Him for the people He has sent to share our day, and entrust Him with tomorrow.

Christian hospitality only accomplishes its true purpose when God becomes our first Guest and is given permanent-resident status. He wants to work with us. He wants the freedom to help us as we offer our hospitality to those He selects. After all, we are in it together.

25

"COME HERE, THAT YOU MAY EAT"

The midmorning sun was probably bright as Boaz stepped through the doorway of his home and started down the dusty road that led to his field. This field would likely have been part of his inheritance as a member of the tribe of Judah. This was the way his agrarian fathers would have traveled as they supervised the harvest in the field toward which Boaz was walking. Bethlehem was a nice village to live in, but during the days of planting and harvest, Boaz would have wanted to leave its quiet streets and to spend his days in the fields that lay outside its boundaries.

As he walked toward his field that day, he could have been thinking of many things. The years of famine had passed, and the harvest now in progress could have caused him to raise heartfelt praise to Jehovah. Boaz had remained in Bethlehem during the years of famine. He well knew the distress of working barren fields—yet God had blessed him. He was one of the leading citizens in his village.

Possibly, Boaz went by the field of his kinsman Elimelech. Elimelech had not stayed in Bethlehem during the years of famine but had gone in search of a more prosperous place in the land of Moab.

Recently there had been quite a stir in Bethlehem. Naomi, the wife of Elimelech, had returned from the land of Moab

alone. Both of her sons and her husband were buried in that
heathen land. Boaz had been told that the Moabite wife of one
of the sons had come back with Naomi. He would have realized
this was a difficult decision for the young woman and that it
would continue to be difficult for her as she lived in Bethlehem.
Boaz would also have known that the fields of Elimelech could
be redeemed by a kinsman. This, however, was not his problem,
for there was a kinsman who was a nearer relative then he.

Boaz may or may not have been thinking of Naomi's return
as he continued toward his harvest field that morning. As he
neared the field, his thoughts, like that of any successful hus-
bandman, would have turned to the work at hand. The harvest
was going well. His servant who supervised the reapers looked
after his interests with care. Boaz could have stayed in his cool
home in Bethlehem, but this would not have appealed to him.
He was a man who liked to supervise his own interests. He pre-
ferred to watch the progress of the harvest. He wanted to know
those who worked in his fields, and he chose to come and share
the noon meal that he provided for his workers to eat under the
shelter he had constructed for their comfort. I feel certain that
those who did the reaping considered Boaz a fair and good
master.

As he approached, surveying his workers, he noticed a young
woman picking up the grain that the reapers had missed. This
was not unusual. The law of Israel required that this be permitted. Boaz would have had other gleaners in his fields as
well, those who lived on the edge of poverty, picking a meager
living off the fields that belonged to other people.

This woman, however, caught his attention. She was young,
probably young enough to be his daughter. She certainly did
not look like the other gleaners. Her background had not prepared her for manual labor. Her shoulders would not yet be
bent under the newly acquired load of poverty. Her demeanor

would have pleased a man such as Boaz. He inquired of his servant, "Whose young woman is this?" (Ruth 2:5).

"She is the young Moabite woman who returned with Naomi from the land of Moab," was the reply (2:6).

The servant quickly gave his master an account of how she had come to be in his field. "Please let me glean and gather after the reapers among the sheaves," she had requested. "Thus she came and has remained from the morning until now; she has been sitting in the house for a little while" (2:7).

Boaz moved through his field, stopping only to instruct his workers to do no harm to this newcomer and to say that she would share the water that was drawn for their refreshment. What were Boaz's thoughts as he walked toward the Moabite woman? Even in the wildest flights of my imagination I cannot believe that Boaz had any idea that God had sent Ruth to be his bride. She was a Moabite—a Gentile. She was also a young woman. Her father-in-law, Elimelech, had probably been Boaz's peer. I have to believe that he extended his hospitality to Ruth that day because of her need. He appreciated her willingness to perform a lowly task in order to care for Naomi.

Boaz was a man of God who saw a need that he could fill. So he said to the Moabite who was gleaning in his field, "Listen carefully, my daughter. Do not go to glean in another field; furthermore, do not go on from this one, but stay here with my maids. Let your eyes be on the field which they reap, and go after them. Indeed, I have commanded the servants not to touch you. When you are thirsty, go to the water jars and drink from what the servants draw" (2:8-9).

Ruth's reaction to this generous offer speaks for itself. "Why have I found favor in your sight that you should take notice of me, since I am a foreigner?" (2:10) she asked. Could it be that Ruth had felt the sting of rejection by others in Bethlehem? Was this gracious act of Boaz made to seem even better because of her longing to be accepted by these people whom she had declared "shall be my people" (1:16)? Boaz's words sank deeply into her heart, bringing great comfort—possibly the first encouragement she had known since coming to her newly adopted land.

Ruth needed to hear these words of encouragement from the kind Boaz. "May the LORD reward your work, and your wages be full from the LORD, the God of Israel, under whose wings you have come to seek refuge" (2:12). After Ruth had expressed her humble thankfulness to Boaz, they would both have returned to their work, she to her gleaning and he to the supervising of the harvest.

As he worked, Boaz was still mindful of this special gleaner. I am sure he glanced her way often during the remainder of the morning. He found her diligent, and her behavior was above reproach. He wanted to do more to help this young woman, so he proceeded to meet her next need. His invitation was gracious, and it was explicit: "Come here, that you may eat of the bread and dip your piece of bread in the vinegar" (Ruth 2:14). There was no mistaking his intent. She was to sit down at his table and to eat the food that he would provide. Not only did he include her in the meal that he provided for his workers, but he also waited on her himself. The narrative says, "He served her roasted grain, and she ate and was satisfied and had some left."

"Leftovers" are sometimes frowned on by those who live in the midst of plenty, but to this poverty-stricken widow of Moab they were a much appreciated gift. They would be used to meet the need of Naomi.

A simple meal had been shared at the edge of a harvest field—an insignificant event—but it was one of Boaz's first steps toward a blessing that God had prepared for him. Boaz would not have been required to meet the needs of this gleaner in the more perfect way that he chose to. All the law required was that she be allowed to glean. He chose to go beyond the requirements of law and to offer true hospitality to the needy one that God sent to his field.

When God chooses to bring across our path someone needy, who by the circumstances of life has been stripped of his possessions, possibly a stranger in our country, how do we react? Like Boaz, do we extend hospitality graciously? Do we speak kindly, making sure that we give comfort? Do we "roast enough grain" so that there will be leftovers to share? Do our actions assure his understanding that our interest is genuine?

Whether God chooses to allow the "gleaners" He sends into our lives to meet a need for us—as He chose that Ruth later met a need in the life of Boaz—should not be our consideration. When God sends our "gleaners," it is our privilege to help meet their needs through our ministry of hospitality. This is part of the sacrifice of love that we can offer to our heavenly Father who has abundantly provided our needs. Like Boaz, our concern should be to bring comfort to the persons involved as we minister to their material needs. When we consider God's love to us, we should find it easy to say to these people, "Come here, that you may eat."

26

A GREAT HOSTESS

She must have been quite a lady—I would have liked to have her for a friend. The Scripture does not give her name; it merely refers to her as a "great woman" (2 Kings 4:8, KJV). This would mean that she was prosperous, a wealthy lady. The story clearly shows that she had great wisdom and spiritual discernment to complement her material prosperity. She was truly a great lady through and through.

Her home was in Shunem. Today, Shunem is not a place you would choose for a vacation, but in the days of Elisha the prophet it seems to have been one of the bright spots in Israel. We know from the text that it was an agricultural village. Even though Baal worship abounded in Israel at this time, the village of Shunem was blessed with some residents who still worshiped Jehovah. Historians tell us that Shunem was on the edge of the rich Plain of Esdraelon, not far from the summer palace of the ungodly Queen Jezebel, wife of wicked King Ahab.

What prompted Elisha's visit to Shunem we are not told. In all probability it would not be a town he would often travel through. It would have been about twenty miles out of the way if he was going from Carmel to Samaria, a route he is thought to have traveled fairly regularly. Elisha would not have had reason to go to the palace of Queen Jezebel, we are quite sure, for he did not enjoy the favor of either the king or queen. All we know is that "Elisha passed over to Shunem" (2 Kings 4:8). The village of Shunem was not large, and the arrival of a prophet was most likely an exciting event. The great lady of Shunem did not miss her opportunity to minister to this servant of God when he came to town. We are told, "She persuaded him to eat food" (4:8). Why did she have to "persuade" him? We can only guess. Possibly the humble prophet was not sure he would enjoy himself in this wealthy home. Or could her feminine gender have caused him to hesitate? The prophet had to be careful, for there were those who were looking for ways to destroy his credibility. Maybe he was just intent on an errand that he had to perform and did not want to be delayed. All we really know is that this great lady succeeded in getting him to accept her hospitality.

The food was sure to have been good. She was a person who would have wanted to give her best to the prophet of Jehovah. The companionship of this lady and her elderly husband must have been special, too. Elisha had a good time, for the Bible next informs us, "As often as he passed by, he turned in there to eat food" (4:8). The "turned in" is believed by some students of Scripture to mean that he went out of his way to visit this couple.

Why would the busy prophet take time to go visit this Shunammite family? To eat, we are told—even prophets must have food. We can only speculate on the other reasons for his regular visits. It could be that there were not many families in Israel at that time whose hearts were set to follow Jehovah, and the prophet longed for and needed the encouragement that this lady and her husband gave him. Here were people who understood that at times he needed to be quiet before God and that at other times he needed the companionship of those who loved his God.

This woman is to me a living illustration of King Lemuel's virtuous woman (see Proverbs 31:10-31), and she had the wisdom to understand the needs of Jehovah's prophet. After Elisha had visited her a few times, a plan began to form in her mind. It was a good plan. She carefully worked out the details of it before she presented it to her husband. This was the request she made: "Please, let us make a little walled upper chamber and let us set a bed for him there, and a table and a chair and a lampstand; and it shall be, when he comes to us, that he can turn in there" (2 Kings 4:10). She wanted a room built for the prophet upon the flat roof of their home—a private "penthouse" with an outside stairway so that Elisha could come and go freely. It was to be a place where he could feel at home. It would be his room.

By the standards of her day, this prophet's room was to be well furnished. A sleeping chamber did not usually have a table, but she would have one in this special guest room. A stool would not do. There must be a chair, a seat of honor for God's prophet. There would be a lampstand for light and a comfortable bed for rest. What a good time she must have had "dressing up" the prophet's chamber, creating a comfortable home for Elisha to enjoy.

She worked without thought of reward. This great lady was a content person. People who really concern themselves with meeting the needs of others do not have time to worry about what they do not have. The childless Israelite woman had her priorities in order. She was ministering to God's servant as a way of expressing her love to Jehovah, her God. The fact that God chose to reward her loving work with an unexpected, unasked-for son must have only increased her desire to serve Him.

What can we learn from this great lady? What lessons in hospitality does she teach us? First, she knew that God's servant was in town and that he had a need. Sometimes we do not keep track of things like that. If we want to enjoy the blessings of hospitality to God's special servants, we will have to keep aware of what is going on around us. We can only meet needs after we find out what they are.

The woman also had discernment as to who was truly God's servant. At the time of Elisha, many false prophets were in Israel; but this lady recognized Elisha to be a "holy man of God" (4:9). We will need to know the marks of a true servant of God so that we do not make a mistake in offering hospitality (see chapter 16, "No Vacancy," for help with this).

The Shunammite hostess was persuasive. She prevailed upon Elisha to be her guest. Often God's servants find it difficult to be on the receiving end of things. Sometimes it takes tactful persuasion to convince them that we really do want them to be our guests. We may need to assure them that we will allow them the study time they need and that we do understand that they have the same human needs that we do.

After persuading God's servants to accept our invitation, we need to follow the example of the great lady by making them feel so much at home that they will want to "turn in" again when they are in our area. It is hoped we will succeed as well as she did, that they will go out of their way to enjoy fellowship with us.

Not many of us can build a special "penthouse" for God's servants, but many of us can have a well-appointed room that will provide needed privacy, and we can be available to encourage them in their work. The great woman of Shunem knew how to practice the kind of hospitality that God intended when he told us to be hospitable, and God rewarded her with an unexpected blessing because she met the need of His prophet.

27

I'LL PREPARE A FEAST

Esther, the Jewish queen of King Ahasuerus, was faced with a problem. God's people were in danger of extermination by indirect order of her husband. What could she do to save them? Esther was well aware of what would happen to a queen who displeased her husband. Her predecessor had been banished from the place when she did not please this king. How could Esther gain the king's favor so that he would listen to her request?

She used a good method—she prepared a feast. In fact, she gave two feasts before she presented her desire to the king. God used her hospitality to gain the favor of this king and to save her people from the sentence of death.

Although I seriously doubt that you or I will be given a situation to deal with as serious as Queen Esther's, I do believe that God can use the feasts we prepare to further His work. It is a well-accepted fact that people are more amiable and cooperative when they have been well fed. If this were not true, there would not be all those banquets to raise money for "worthy causes." They work!

Could it be that God wants you to prepare a feast to bring together people whom He wants to work together? As a pastor's wife I have prepared many meals for various committees and boards who needed to explore a new idea or to review an old one. People of different opinions become more willing to relinquish their pet views and seek God's will after they have eaten a good meal around the same table.

Sometimes God directs us to bring together representatives of various Christian groups so that they may cooperate in their efforts to do the work of the ministry. Often these people do not know each other. Prepare a feast—let them get acquainted over the dinner table. They may find that they do not need to compete with each other. In fact, because they have similar goals they may discover that by cooperating they can all do a better job.

When God lays a certain need on your heart for one of His projects, ask Him to let you know who might be interested in this undertaking. Prepare a feast and invite these prospects—please inform them of the purpose of your feast when you invite them. When you have feasted together, present them with the facts: this is what has been done; this is what needs to be done; these are some of the ways that the work can be done. Invite your guests to prayerfully consider whether or not this is one of the good works in which God would want them to participate. This is promotion work, and there is nothing wrong with it when you are promoting activities that are pleasing to God in a way that is God-honoring.

When Queen Esther went to King Ahasuerus, she risked a great deal. She was jeopardizing her position as queen and possibly her life to save God's people. She did not go to the king without adequate preparation. Her people had prayed and fasted with her for three days and three nights before she approached him. When she went she was not seeking favor for herself but rather salvation for her people.

When you prepare a feast to promote God's work be sure that you do more than prepare food. Seek God's guidance every step of the way. Prepare your feast with prayer. Make sure that the purpose of this feast is not to bring you glory but that it is really prepared to bring glory to God. Feasts prepared in prayer for the glory of God can bring salvation to people.

However, sometimes when we have planned with right motives and have prayed asking God's blessing, things do not go the way we think they should. What happens then? If you have done the work for the Lord, you do not need to be hurt or offended if your guests change "your" plans or discard them. God will bring good out of your good work, and it is not necessary for us to see all the results now or ever. After all, it is His work, not ours. Psalm 119:165 tells us:

> Those who love Thy law have great peace,
> And nothing causes them to stumble.

If we have soaked up God's word and have asked God's direction as we have done our preparation, we do not need to stumble into Satan's trap of self-pity if things do not go our way. It is God's way that we are interested in, and He will redeem our work in His way.

However, many times our experience will be like that of Queen Esther. God will bless the feast by giving us receptive guests who will receive us as God's messengers and respond. God uses feasts—do not overlook the possibility that God may be asking you to prepare a feast to present His work to someone who is in the position of being able to help that work.

God also uses feasts to gain the attention of people who need Him as Savior. If God has laid on your heart the burden for an unsaved person or a group of people, consider the possibility of inviting them to a feast. We met one of our closest friends this way. He was the father of a playmate of our son. We invited this family to share our Thanksgiving feast even though we had never met the father. God used this to begin to gain this man's attention. The next Easter Sunday he entered God's family by being born again. His interest began with our simply inviting him to share a feast with us.

All Israel remembers Queen Esther and the feast she prepared as a way to help save her people from physical death. Will anyone have reason to remember that they were saved from spiritual death because you prepared a feast?

28

THERE IS ROOM IN THE STABLE

"And she [Mary] gave birth to her first-born son; and she wrapped Him in cloths, and laid Him in a manger, because there was no room for them in the inn" (Luke 2:7).

Luke alone tells of the circumstances of the birth of Jesus. Over the years I have heard much said, mostly derogatory, about the innkeeper of Bethlehem, but none of it comes from God's Word. He is not even spoken of there. Yet reason tells us that there was such a person, and tradition causes us to assume that this innkeeper was a man. Will you join me as I try to imagine what the night of Nativity was like for this businessman of Bethlehem?

Remember as you read that this is strictly a journey into what might have happened. God chose not to give us the details of this event. We do not even know for sure if the stable in which Jesus Christ was born belonged to the inn.

The shadows of evening were long in the street outside the inn in Bethlehem. Behind the closed door, the innkeeper sat down at last. He stretched a bit as he mused—he would have no trouble meeting the new tax that Caesar Augustus had levied. Every available spot in the inn was occupied. This meant revenue for him—hard earned income. He watched the descendants of King David spread out pallets side by side on the floor. He had done his best to meet the needs of these travelers. He could not do any more. There was no more room in his inn.

The innkeeper sighed, a tired but satisfied sigh, the kind that comes so naturally when you rest after having completed your work. Soon this rest was interrupted by someone at the door. He arose to answer the call—to tell whoever it was that he could not help them. His inn was full. His resources were all used up, or so he thought.

As he opened the door, in the twilight of Bethlehem stood Joseph of Nazareth. The evening light illuminated Mary, just a step or two behind him. Even the tired innkeeper with no room left could understand that here was a real need. Obviously the young woman standing at his doorway was about to become a mother. One cannot just shut the door on such a person—so he did what he could. He invited them to stay in the stable.

Carved out of the side of the hill, the stable was free of drafts and reasonably warm. There was clean straw and the tired lady about to give birth to a child could rest there as his guest. It was all he had left to offer, and he offered it willingly. He had no way of knowing that the Child about to be born was to be the Messiah that Israel longed for. All that the innkeeper saw was a need, and he did what he could to be of help.

Do not condemn the innkeeper. If God had wanted His son to be born in the inn, He could have arranged for Mary and Joseph to arrive in Bethlehem before the last spot on that inn floor had been filled by someone else's pallet. God's arrangement was just right to meet the need of Mary and her Son. The stable provided the quiet atmosphere that Mary needed for rest after their tiring journey. It also gave privacy during the time of birth. Thank God for the stable—it was just right!

We who are used to our innerspring mattresses may cringe, but my grandmother slept on a straw tick, as a child. I, also, have some very pleasant memories of curling up on an old quilt that had been laid over the sweet-smelling hay in my father's haymow—it was a delightful place to read or daydream on a nice rainy day. God had arranged just the right set of circumstances to insure that Mary's needs that night would be well cared for.

Real or imaginary, the "innkeeper tradition" teaches a biblical truth about hospitality. God will sometimes choose to send a guest to us when we think all our resources are used up. If the need is real, and the guest is sent from God, He also has a creative solution to the problems that come along with the guest. What we need to do when this happens is to ask for His wisdom in how to best minister to this guest.

A number of years ago, God illustrated this truth for me. We were preparing to leave on a three-week trip early Monday morning. These were our prefreezer days, and by careful planning we had eaten most of the food in the refrigerator by Saturday night. There was just enough left to feed the four of us on Sunday. Early that Sunday morning we received a telephone call informing us that one of our church missionary families had just arrived home on furlough and that they would be in our morning worship service. They would like to spend the afternoon with us if possible. This meant Sunday dinner. The bank account could not endure taking ten of us out to dinner, and at that time the supermarkets were closed on Sunday.

I was not happy to do what I had to do that day. From the local Seven-Eleven store I bought rolls, cold cuts, cheese, chips and dip, along with ice cream for dessert. This was not what I wanted to give our friends for their first stateside meal, but it was all that I could do. I was prepared to apologize for my offering.

However, God had a lesson for me that day—the best I could do was just right. It was, in fact, a very special treat for our guests. These were just the foods that they had been waiting to have when they got home. In their place of service, cold cuts, good cheese, and chips and dip were not available, and ice cream was a very rare treat.

God knew the right menu for these four missionary children

and their parents. He also knew it was not what I would have elected to serve, so He made just the right set of circumstances to make it necessary for me to produce what they most wanted. A meal is a small thing, but I have a God who is interested in making even small things just right.

When we are cooperating with God in the ministry of hospitality, there will be times when we think that we have no more room, food, or strength. But if God sends the guest, you can be sure that He knows of resources you have overlooked. He never asks us to give what we do not have.

The very same God who created the right circumstances to insure quietness and privacy for Mary, can and will direct you in your hospitality. Sometimes this direction will come in the form of what seem like impossible circumstances. When this happens, rejoice—for this is when biblical hospitality can become high adventure, and we are given amazing glimpses into the creativity of our God.

29

THE NIGHT VISITOR

Night is a private time, even today when electricity illuminates the darkness. It is the time that we withdraw from the world at large and close the doors of our dwelling places. It is our own time to rest. In Jerusalem during the days that God walked on earth in the person of Jesus Christ, night was made even more private by virtue of Jewish superstitions concerning the evils of darkness.

In the third chapter of John's gospel, the apostle tells of a night visitor. Jesus had withdrawn from the busy ministry of the day to a private place, probably the home of a friend. We know that His days during this time of Passover had been full, but now it was night—the time for rest.

There were no lights to illuminate the street as the Pharisee Nicodemus slipped from his house into the dark of the night. He was on his way to make a most important visit. This was not a social call, for social calls were made during the daylight hours. Nicodemus had decided to find out about this man Jesus for himself. He knew that this was a call that could cause trouble for him with his colleagues on the Jewish council, if it was discovered. Knowing this, Nicodemus elected to come to Jesus under the cover of darkness, thus interrupting this new teacher's private rest time.

Nicodemus made this night visit because of a desire for truth.

He must have felt compelled to know more about this carpenter's son who had come into the Temple and had removed those who bought and sold the sacrificial animals there. He had probably been present when Jesus had been questioned about His right to clear the Temple of its commercial enterprises and had been puzzled by the answer Jesus had given. Possibly Nicodemus was aware that this Jesus was credited with changing water into wine at a wedding in Cana, and he had heard many reports of miracles during the Passover week.

All of this had perplexed the well-to-do, highly educated Pharisee, who considered himself an authority on the God of his father Abraham. Over the days of Passover, more and more questions had arisen to make Nicodemus unsure of just what was the truth. How could this carpenter from Nazareth fit into God's prophecy concerning Israel? However, Nicodemus was an honest man, and he had come to believe that this man was sent from God. His works seemed to demand that Nicodemus accept this fact.

This belief had become so strong that Nicodemus was willing to risk his position on the council to find out just how this man fit into God's plan. He had made the effort to find out where he might go under the cover of night to find the new teacher who had no home of His own in the city.

We may imagine that this visit took Nicodemus into a part of Jerusalem where he was not often found. As a wealthy member of the Sanhedrin, Nicodemus would have lived in the better part of Jerusalem. Because most of Jesus' early followers came from the poorer working class, Nicodemus may well have traveled unfamiliar and possibly dangerous streets to make his night call. In spite of all these difficulties Nicodemus was willing to come, uninvited, to interrupt the private rest time of Jesus. He had a need that was more important than social custom.

When we receive night visitors, they come with needs and they want truth. They come confused in their thinking, and they want help badly enough to break the rules of society. How should these seekers be received into our private time of rest? Often it is inconvenient and sometimes downright disruptive to receive a call from a night visitor. How can we best minister to the needs of these night intruders? Jesus gives us an example to follow in the way that He ministered to Nicodemus.

There is no record of social small talk on the part of Jesus in this text (John 3:2-3). Listen to the opening exchange. Nicodemus began by saying, " 'Rabbi, we know that You have come from God as a teacher; for no one can do these signs that You do unless God is with him.' Jesus answered and said to him, 'Truly, truly, I say to you, unless one is born again, he cannot see the kingdom of God.' "

These two statements do not really seem to relate to each other. Jesus did not agree or disagree with Nicodemus's statement. Instead, He went directly to the man's need. Jesus, it seems, was implying that Nicodemus must have believed he could get the answers he needed by coming to Him. He did not waste time talking about who He was, but got right to Nicodemus's problem. "Nicodemus, you need to be born again." Jesus knew the risk that Nicodemus took by coming to see Him, and He got right down to the business of stating the man's need.

When people trust us enough to come into our private night, our response should be like Jesus'—we should do what we can to discern their real need as quickly as possible. We, of course, do not know the hearts of men as our Master does, and we may have to probe a little to identify their need. Often they cannot tell us what their real need is, for, like Nicodemus, they do not know. Our obligation is to rely on the wisdom of God to discover this need and to help them deal with it.

Once Jesus stated the need, He took time to make sure Nicodemus understood what his need was. He used examples from life, things like birth and wind. He went to the Scriptures, with which Nicodemus was fully acquainted, concerning Moses and the wilderness serpent. Jesus made sure that Nicodemus recognized his real need, the need for a spiritual birth.

The fact that Nicodemus was a leader in Israel did not intimidate Jesus, though his lack of spiritual perception seemed to amaze Him. When we invite God to send into our lives people who have needs, we may be surprised at those who show up. People come from all walks of life, have all kinds of needs, and God equips us to minister to those needs if we are willing to let Him work through us. Sometimes our ministry will even extend to those who have authority over us in our daily lives.

Each person that God sends us must be treated with consideration. Like Jesus, we may sometimes be amazed at people's lack of understanding of spiritual truth. We must, therefore, make sure that we use language they can understand so they will have the opportunity to respond to God's truth if they choose to do so.

As a Pharisee, Nicodemus was a keeper of the law. He would have worked hard to keep every jot and tittle of Jewish law, for the Pharisees viewed their God as a judge. Jesus needed to correct Nicodemus's one-sided view of God. By doing so He gave us the most beautiful dissertation on God's love ever recorded. Jesus explained a loving and yet just God to Nicodemus in this way:

> "For God so loved the world, that He gave His only begotten Son, that whoever believes in Him should not perish, but have eternal life. For God did not send the Son into the world to judge the world; but that the world should be saved through Him. He who believes in Him is not judged; he who does not believe has been judged already, because he has not believed in the name of the only begotten Son of God" (John 3:16-18).

When night visitors come to us we must make sure they understand that God's desire is not to condemn them but to deliver them from condemnation. They must know that they will be condemned only if they choose to be—by rejection of God's redemption.

After Jesus made sure that Nicodemus knew his own need and that he knew who God was, He proceeded to show him what man is. He defined the struggle between good and evil in terms of light and darkness. Nicodemus could understand these figures of speech for he had just come to Jesus under cover of darkness.

We need to explain to our troubled visitors the struggle that goes on in the heart of every man who seeks truth. This fear of exposure that is common to sinful man—and the release and freedom that come when we yield to the light of God's truth— must be made clear.

With this, the dialogue that John records between Jesus and Nicodemus closes. John does not choose to give us Nicodemus's response to the truth Jesus presented to him. Maybe this is because Nicodemus made no visible response on that dark night. If the whole matter were left there we could think that the interview was a failure. Jesus had missed the rest that His tired human body needed. Nicodemus, under cover of darkness, went back to his home. It was all over. Maybe he felt better— or maybe worse because of this risk that he had taken. We are not told.

However, later this same Nicodemus asked a question openly of his fellow Pharisees when they were seeking to destroy Jesus: "Does our law condemn a man without first hearing him to find out what he is doing?" (John 7:51, NIV). It was just a question, but it indicates that Nicodemus had not forgotten his interview with the Son of God.

In John 19:39-40, we find Nicodemus along with Joseph of Arimathea generously caring for the burial of the crucified Messiah. This was certainly a public expression of his commitment to Jesus Christ. He was no longer hiding under the cover of night.

Sometimes we too will see little response from our night visitors. We may be tempted to think that our time has been wasted. This is when we need to remember that our commission is to present the message of God faithfully and clearly with compassion. The outcome of our interview must be entrusted to God who has promised that His message will bear its fruit in its own season.

30

DINNER AT SIMON'S

Simon stood at a distance, listening. He was not planning to be part of the crowd of people who had gathered around the new rabbi—after all Simon was a Pharisee, a keeper of the law. Yet, he was curious about this teacher whom the people followed.

Only yesterday Simon had heard that Jesus was credited with disrupting a burial procession. It was not the disruption that bothered him—it was the method of disruption. The story as it was told him declared that this teacher had raised the dead boy—had actually given him life after death. Those who reported the happening were saying, "A great prophet had arisen among us!" and, "God has visited His people" (Luke 7:16).

So Simon now stood apart from the crowd, listening, trying to decide if this man really was a "great prophet." There was nothing comely about Him that would cause this following He enjoyed. Yet He had an air of authority that could be felt as He spoke. Simon continued to listen.

Two messengers then came to the teacher from John the Baptist, who was in Herod's prison. "Are You the one who is coming," they asked, "or do we look for someone else?" (Luke 7:20).

The teacher's answer was in the manner of the rabbis, an answer that left the decision with the questioner. "Go," he said, "and report to John what you have seen and heard: the BLIND RECEIVE SIGHT, the lame walk, the lepers are cleansed, and the deaf hear, the dead are raised up, the POOR HAVE THE GOSPEL PREACHED TO THEM. And blessed is he who keeps from stumbling over Me" (Luke 7:22-23).

Simon pondered the answer, half listening to the Master's words to the multitude, words about John the Baptist. This was a man that Simon did not want to think about. As a Pharisee he had rejected the message of the wilderness prophet who had stirred up the people with his teaching of repentance. As a Pharisee who kept the law, Simon had no need of repentance. Was this new teacher going to cause more trouble for them?

The dinner hour was drawing near as Simon began to move through the crowd. The people who had been listening to the rabbi parted to allow him to approach their new teacher. Simon's schooling in the Talmud dictated his action now, for he was a keeper of law. Rabbinic custom compelled him to extend an invitation to this new teacher to come and dine with him.

Simon was troubled as he walked with his guest through the streets of the city to the door of his home. Was this man really a prophet? If so, why did He spend His time with publicans and sinners? Why was He not sitting in the council? Simon glanced over his shoulder as they approached his doorway. A woman of the street had followed them. Simon closed his eyes and did not open them until he had turned his head. It was not proper for him, a Pharisee, to contemplate such a person. He had noticed her earlier in the crowd that had surrounded his guest.

They entered the house. The cool room was a welcome relief after an afternoon under the hot sun. The table was laid, ready for them to eat. The couches on which they would recline as they ate stood waiting to be occupied. The steward seated Rabbi Jesus with his back to the doorway. Simon reclined to the right of his guest. As was the custom of the day, he lay on his side with one elbow on the table, his feet stretched out behind him.

From his position at the table Simon could see the doorway
through which they had just entered.

His face suddenly mirrored the shock that he felt. There in
his dining room, behind his guest, stood the woman of the
street—the one he had seen following them. How did she gain
access to his house? Had she slipped in while the servants were
busy? Or had she bribed one of them to let her in?

His first inclination was to call a servant to remove her
quickly, but then a thought crossed his mind. If this guest of his
was a prophet, He would surely know what this woman was.
No rabbi would have any dealings with such a sinner in public.
Here was the test Simon needed to see if this man was the
prophet that the people claimed Him to be. Simon waited.

The woman moved silently until she stood behind the couch
of his guest. Suddenly, to Simon's horror, she burst into tears
that flowed like a fountain onto the travel-stained feet of the
teacher. She was standing behind the rabbi, weeping and wiping
the tears from His feet with her long hair. Then she bent and
began to kiss His feet and to anoint them with the oil that, as
was the custom of women, she carried in a little vial around her
neck.

Simon recoiled at the sight. How could this rabbi allow such
a woman to touch Him? What was He thinking? What would
He do now? Jesus answered his unspoken questions in a manner befitting a rabbi:

" 'Simon, I have something to say to you.'

[Simon wanted and needed to hear what Jesus would say in
order to make up his mind about this man.]

" 'Say it, Teacher,' [was his quick reply.]

" 'A certain moneylender had two debtors: one owed five
hundred denarii, and the other fifty. When they were unable to
repay, he graciously forgave them both. Which of them therefore will love him more?'

"Simon answered and said, 'I suppose the one whom he for-

gave more.' And [Jesus] said to him, 'You have judged correctly.' And turning toward the woman, He said to Simon, 'Do
you see this woman? I entered your house; you gave Me no
water for My feet, but she has wet My feet with her tears, and
wiped them with her hair. You gave Me no kiss; but she, since
the time I came in, has not ceased to kiss My feet. You did not
anoint My head with oil, but she anointed My feet with per-
fume. For this reason I say to you, her sins, which were many,
have been forgiven, for she loved much; but he who is forgiven
little, loves little' " (Luke 7:40-47).

Simon now sat in silence, having no answer for his guest. This
rabbi by use of an illustration had silenced him. Jesus had not
been rude in His answer. He in fact had gently shown His host
that His mission on this earth was to meet the needs of sinners,
not to worry about the ceremonial law that the Pharisees so
zealously claimed to keep. He had also shown Simon that, for
all his zeal to keep ritual, he had fallen short of his mark by not
providing his guest with the required foot washing.

Jesus had graciously shown Simon that He could meet the
need and accept the adoration of one who had much to be forgiven. But He had also said that He could and would forgive
the one who owed little. He had taken the time to show His host
that he was not without sin and that his sin could be forgiven.

If Jesus is resident in our Christian homes, people will come,
some invited, some uninvited. They will come to receive His
love and to show their love to Him. Some will also come to try
to discredit Him. Jesus promised, "And I, if I be lifted up from
the earth, will draw all men to Myself" (John 12:32). This
includes the Simons who do not know that they are sinners, the
women of the street (people with whom it is not proper to associate), and the multitude of people that fall between these two
extremes.

How do you react when you receive these guests? Jesus Christ
has set a pattern for us. For the Simons who come, our ministry

is to politely show them their need of salvation—to bring them to the place where they can see clearly that they are sinners. Following this, we must help them to understand that the Master forgives those who "owe little" (by human standards) as well as those who "owe much."

At the other end of the spectrum, the down-and-out sinner already knows his state. The message here can begin with the forgiveness that is available for his great debt of sin of which he is already aware.

Our obligation is to present the message, tailor-made, to each individual that comes—whether he is a Simon or a woman of the street. When we have done that, we can commit our guest to the gracious ministry of the Holy Spirit who will make the truth real to them.

31

A SOLDIER OBEYS

Cornelius was a man of authority, a Roman centurion, who was used to commanding men. His duty assignment was the city of Caesarea. His responsibilities there probably included keeping order in the city, the guarding of prisoners, and the execution of those who were sentenced to die by Roman law. In spite of his position of leadership in the Roman army, this Italian officer was "well spoken of by the entire nation of the Jews" (Acts 10:22). Cornelius, it seems, had done his homework very well. We can only guess how this Gentile may have arrived at the place where we first meet him in the tenth chapter of the book of Acts.

Could it be that, since he was assigned to a city having a large Jewish population, he had made a study of the religion and lifestyle of the Jews? Cornelius was an honest man, and at some point in his life he had decided to direct his worship toward the God who was worshiped by these Hebrew residents of Caesarea. This decision probably would have caused him to abandon the idols of the Gentiles and to remove images from his home.

Cornelius's faith is attested by the fact that he had instructed his entire household in the fear of the true God. We are told that he went even further with his allegiance to God by giving love gifts (alms) to the Jewish people. He was willing to let his faith reach into his pocketbook.

He did not hide his devotion to Jehovah, for he regularly observed the Jewish hours of prayer. In spite of all this, it seems apparent that Cornelius was not a Jewish proselyte. He had not joined the synagogue, where he could have worshiped in the area reserved for the Gentiles. Instead, he chose to worship the true God in his own home.

It was during his regular prayer hour, at about three o'clock in the afternoon, that Cornelius received a heavenly visitor in a vision. The angel of God came to him. He had a message for Cornelius, a command for him to obey. The angel told him: "Your prayers and alms have ascended as a memorial before God. And now dispatch some men to Joppa, and send for a man named Simon, who is also called Peter: he is staying with a certain tanner named Simon, whose house is by the sea" (Acts 10:4b-6).

We are not told what Cornelius had been praying about prior to this vision. His worship may have been in the form of praise, or possibly it was petition. Could he have asked God for direction about how to serve Him more perfectly? The Bible does not choose to tell the nature of Cornelius's prayer, but the angel's message implies that Cornelius had been praying for additional understanding of God's will and purpose.

Here in Acts 10 God gives a picture of an obedient man. When he was told to send for Peter, he did so. That may sound like an easy command for Cornelius to obey, but was it?

Cornelius would have known that Jewish law must be bent to the breaking point for Peter, a Jew, to accept the invitation to come to his house. Also, the address given could have caused a problem for Cornelius. A tanner was not considered a part of elite society in that day. The Jewish laws of purification could hardly be kept by a tanner. Those who held that occupation were required to carry on their business outside the city limits. Cornelius, historians point out, bore the name of a distinguished family in the Roman Empire. He would have made his friends

among those who lived in the better parts of any city. Could
God really want him to ask a man who was lodging with a
tanner to visit him?

I find it interesting that God chose a Roman soldier to dem-
onstrate that His message of salvation was for the Gentiles as
well as the Jews. Cornelius not only knew how to give commands; as a good soldier he had also learned how to obey
commands from his superiors. When God commanded Cornelius to cross economic, social, and national barriers, he
obeyed immediately, no questions asked. He did not present a
better plan or a reason why he could not involve himself with
an exfisherman who was lodging with a tanner. He chose two
of his household slaves and a devout soldier (one who also believed in the God of Israel) to fetch this guest whom God had
promised would show him what he needed to do to perfect his
faith.

We have just a few hints of what Cornelius did in the four
days before the men returned. In Acts 10:24 we are told that
when Peter and his party entered the city of Caesarea, they
found Cornelius waiting for them. He had expected them to
come, in spite of the cultural barriers he knew were present.
He had believed God enough to be watching for their arrival.
He also believed that Peter would obey God's command and
come across those barriers to present God's message to him. But
waiting was not the only activity of Cornelius during those days.
He gave invitations (or possibly commands) to his relatives
and close friends to come and hear what God's servant Peter
would have to tell them.

Cornelius was using his home for his God. It was a place
where people could come to have their spiritual needs met. This
is a picture of godly hospitality. Cornelius was willing to share
his home and his special messenger from God with others. Because of this obedience, God had great blessings for him.

When I think of Cornelius, I think of a man singled out by

God to be a "forerunner." He was used of God to first illustrate to all men that salvation was for Gentiles as well as Jews. God asked him to do some hard things, and he willingly obeyed. When God asks us to cross economic, social, racial, or national barriers, are we as willing to obey as Cornelius was? Our obedience in these areas shows those who come to us for help and those who watch us from afar "that God is not one to show partiality, but in every nation the man who fears Him and does what is right, is welcome to Him" (Acts 10:34b-35). God's welcome is clear—is ours? Like Cornelius, can you welcome someone who comes from the wrong side of town? Like Peter, can you cross the barriers of your tradition to present the love of Christ? Can you invite the person that God is sending to be your guest?

NOTES

CHAPTER 11

1. Paul Tournier, *Learn to Grow Old* (New York: Harper & Row, 1972), p. 63.

CHAPTER 20

1. Edith Schaeffer, *Hidden Art* (Wheaton, Ill.: Tyndale, 1971), p. 120.

CHAPTER 22

1. Abigail Van Buren, "Dear Abby," *Washington Star*, 23 January 1977.

BIBLIOGRAPHY

Alexander, David, and Alexander, Pat, eds. *Eerdmans' Handbook to the Bible.* Grand Rapids: Eerdmans, 1937.

Edersheim, Alfred. *Old Testament Bible History.* Wilmington, Del.: Assoc. Publishers and Authors, n.d.

Edersheim, Alfred. *The Life and Times of Jesus the Messiah.* 2 vols. 1901. Reprint. Grand Rapids: Eerdmans, 1950.

Farrar, F. W. *The Life and Work of St Paul.* London: Cassell, 1898.

Fowler, Sina Faye. *Food for Fifty.* New York: Wiley, 1937.

Ironside, H. A. *Lectures on the Book of Acts.* New York: Loizeaux, 1943.

Kelly, William. *An Exposition of the Acts of the Apostles.* London: Hammond, 1952.

Lange, John Peter. *A Commentary on the Holy Scriptures.* 25 vols. *Joshua, Judges, Ruth,* vol. 4. c. 1864-80. Reprint. Grand Rapids: Zondervan, n.d.

Mow, Anna B. *So Who's Afraid of Birthdays.* Philadelphia: Lippincott, 1969.

Ockenga, Harold John. *Women Who Made Bible History.* Grand Rapids: Zondervan, 1962.

Rackham, Richard Belward. *The Acts of the Apostles.* Grand Rapids: Baker, 1901.

Schaeffer, Edith. *Hidden Art.* Wheaton, Ill.: Tyndale, 1971.

————. *What Is a Family.* Old Tappan, N.Y.: Revell, 1975.

Tournier, Paul. *Learning to Grow Old.* New York: Harper & Row, 1971.

Trever, G. H. "Cornelius." In *The International Standard Bible Encyclopaedia,* edited by James Orr, 2:721. Grand Rapids: Eerdmans, 1939.

Van Buren, Abigail. "Dear Abby." *Washington Star,* 23 January 1977.

Wiseman, D. J., ed. *The Tyndale Old Testament Commentaries. Judges and Ruth.* Chicago: InterVarsity Press, 1968.